Barbara Cawthorne Crafton

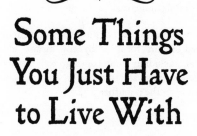

Some Things You Just Have to Live With

Musings on Middle Age

MOREHOUSE PUBLISHING
A Continuum imprint
HARRISBURG • LONDON • NEW YORK

Morehouse Publishing
P.O. Box 1321
Harrisburg, PA 17105

Morehouse Publishing is a Continuum imprint.

Design by Corey Kent

Library of Congress Cataloging-in-Publication Data

Crafton, Barbara Cawthorne.
  Some things you just have to live with : musings on middle age / Barbara Cawthorne Crafton.
    p. cm.
  ISBN 0-8192-1930-4
  1. Middle aged women—Religious life. 2. Christian women—Religious life. 3. Crafton, Barbara Cawthorne. I. Title.
  BV4579.5.C73 2003
  248.8'43—dc21

                                        2003001564

Printed in the United States of America

03 04 05 06 07 08   6 5 4 3 2 1

Contents

This book is
dedicated
in loving memory
of
Caroline Mattern Towt,
1920–2002,
with gratitude
for the honor of being her friend.

O Lord, support us all the day long,
until the shadows lengthen,
and the evening comes,
and the busy world is hushed,
and the fever of life is over,
and our work is done.
Then in thy mercy,
grant us a safe lodging,
and a holy rest,
and peace at the last.

—A Prayer for the Evening,
The Book of Common Prayer

To the Reader

❦

Many things about middle age have surprised me:

That I have returned to old loves, to birds and to the garden, after decades of paying little or no attention to them.

That I have lost energy and really don't mind much.

That I wear less makeup. I always thought I'd need more when I got older, but find instead that more than just a touch makes me look like Elizabeth I toward the end of her reign.

That I can hardly bear to wear high-heeled shoes any more and don't care if I look frumpy.

That I think about death a fair amount and don't mind that, either.

That I'm still capable of petty jealousy. I thought I'd grow out of it.

That time does not exist or, if it does, it's very elastic. I thought half a century would be a long time, and it just isn't.

That I like to exercise, and that I am competitive about it, even though I am never the best at anything.

That I no longer have trouble believing in things that don't make a whole lot of sense. Making sense is highly overrated. I have much less faith in human logic than I did when I was young. And more faith in God.

I still don't know what's going on in this world. I am much less sure about most things than I used to be. But I feel the pull of the love of God all the time, feel it and do not understand, and I don't care nearly so much about not understanding.

The Geranium Farm
2002

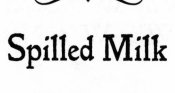

Spilled Milk

Why We're Special.
Why We're Not.

Usually I am leading an orchestra. Something thunderous, with lots of tympani for me to cue, like the second movement of Beethoven's *Ninth Symphony* or the opening bars of *Fanfare for the Common Man*. It's never *Also Sprach Zarathustra*, oddly enough, although the tympani part is so cool in that one—I just don't **like** *Also Sprach Zarathustra*. And it's my orchestra.

I look good. Really good. Younger than I usually look, and a lot thinner, with great hair. My dress is expensive and just severe enough to become an orchestra conductor without overpowering my almost unbelievable beauty. I can tell that the orchestra is impressed with me. This is how I know

I'm daydreaming: In this fantasy, I don't know what I really *do* know about musicians and how easily impressed they are.

Sometimes I'm *not* the conductor. Sometimes I'm the soloist. I look pretty good in that one, too, in a brighter and lower-cut dress, and I send out my voice with a power that makes it seem effortless. My back is straight, my chin is lifted—I have only one chin in this one. My shoulders do not move. I add cadenzas hitherto unimagined, hit notes that the most thoroughly castrated castrato who ever lived could not have sung on his very best day. The conductor is in love with my voice, and perhaps with me: he all but ignores the orchestra, half turning from his podium to watch me sing. Another clue that this is a daydream.

I never tire of it. It comes into my mind unbidden now, after all these years of stoking it: the radio plays something I love and I become the performer—or, rather, the performer becomes *me. I* am the one whose gift holds an audience spellbound. *Is there still time?* I wonder as I drive along. Is there still time for me to become the toast of Broadway? Still time for me to win the Van Cliburn award?

Hell, no. Not if I don't practice or sing regularly or really play the piano at all any more, not after many fallow years of never playing. No, there's no time. Not for me to burst upon the scene and take New York or anywhere else by storm without doing any work. These things must remain the stuff of daydreams. That's fine with me. There's a limit to the number of besotted orchestra conductors we could accommodate around our house. We already have four cats.

But I observe the tug on my soul of being center stage. I see that I long to be the star. I see that I eagerly read my reviews, and fasten on the tiniest of negative criticisms in an agony of hurt feelings. How odd in a grownup.

And how uncomfortable in a Christian. We're supposed to be humble.

I pretend indifference, in a vain attempt to change my innards. Noisily, I don't save my photographs. Couldn't tell you where they are. Surreptitiously, almost unconsciously, though, I tuck most of them away here and there—it is really only the unattractive ones I discard. I may genuinely forget where they are, but one thing is certain: they're around here somewhere. I didn't throw them away.

There's a rowing competition at the gym. Basically, we compete with ourselves: we're trying to row 100,000 meters in one month. There's another level of excellence—200,000 in a month—but I'm aiming for 100,000. Don't think *that* wasn't a hard decision.

So if I go five days a week, for four weeks, that's twenty visits to the gym, and I'll need to row 5,000 meters each time. I can do that.

But I don't go to the gym five times a week. I should, but I don't. I go only three or four times. Sometimes I don't go because I'm tired, even though I know going there always makes me feel energetic. One time I didn't go because I was angry at my husband. That was sensible.

The math changes as the month progresses. I can do 6,000 at a time, maybe. But I fall behind. One day I do 12,000 meters. When I finish, the backs of my thighs hurt so much I can barely walk.

Four days before the end of the month I have rowed 58,000 meters. 42,000 left to go. So if I go each day and row 10,500 meters, I can still do it.

One of the four days is Sunday. That's not going to work.

In the end, I have rowed 62,500.

A computer printout appears on the bulletin board where the staff usually post things about eating vegetables and stretching before workouts. The printout lists the names of all the participants in the rowing challenge. My name won't be on the list, I think glumly as I pass it. I didn't meet the challenge. I stop and study the list, just to rub a little salt in my own wounds.

The printout includes people from lots of gyms, not just ours. The folks from our gym are highlighted in yellow. There aren't that many of them—maybe twenty people participated in the rowing challenge. One guy rowed 422,000 meters. Three rowed over 200,000.

My name *is* on the list, I discover.

With my 62,000 meters. That was nice of them.

Hey, wait—maybe I was the woman who rowed the most!

Nope. Several other women beat me.

Hey, maybe I'm the oldest?

No way to tell.

This must be a sign from God, a reminder that I'm old enough to know better than to grasp at such straws of self-esteem. You don't get on the list just if you won. You get on it just for trying.

Oh.

I get it now.

It's not being the conductor that makes me special. I'm not the conductor.

It's not being the star. I'm not the star.

It's not winning. I didn't win.

It's not standing out in the crowd. I'm not special because I'm in a class by myself.

I'm special because I was in the class. In the game. In the orchestra. In the group. In the human race. In the world, for however brief a moment in its history. Engaged. Trying. Beloved of God. That's all and that's enough.

Oh.

Jesus Wept

❧

At first, I didn't know I was depressed. I thought I was just religious.

I knew I was beyond tired, beyond exhausted. I knew I was out of shape. I knew I was overworked. What I didn't know was that there was any way *not* to be any of those things. But then, part of depression *is* not knowing that things can be other than the way they are. *This is horrible,* you think. *I have always been here and I must stay here. I cannot leave.* Maybe there are little things you can do to make life more livable, you think, but the basics are set.

In my office, a beautiful womblike room with wine-red walls and dark wood and stained-glass windows, I tried to create an oasis of beauty and quiet that would calm and nurture others and might even calm and nurture me. I bought bunches of roses at the corner vegetable stand and arranged them in clear, round bowls of clean water. I lit scented candles, whose tiny flames reflected and multiplied in the facets of their crystal holders. I rocked in the wooden rocking chair. I played the chants of medieval monks and nuns, the music of Bach. Once in a while I played the Beatles, or something by Paul Simon. Not often, though: they reminded me too painfully of the confident young woman I was when those songs were new, and that young woman didn't understand. *Get over it,* she said, dismissively.

I sneaked out the back door of the church and across the street to the chiropractor. *Your shoulders are like a rock,* he said every time. I know. All my muscles were knots of anxious readiness. Readiness for what, I cannot say.

Fourteen, fifteen, sixteen—the heaped-up voice-mail messages filled me with dread. Someone wanting something, someone to whom I owed work, someone reminding me of something I had failed to do. "Save," I pressed, over and over. Save me, I thought sometimes, and sometimes something dark answered that nobody could save me.

My prayer was the weariness of a child exhausted from too much crying. Prayer in the beautiful wine-colored office was prayer blinking back tears, prayer curiously devoid of hope, prayer even more curiously uninterested in its own outcome. I pressed "Save" and prayed to be saved myself. But I began to suspect that I would not be saved until I left my church and my family and my mind and my body—and all the other things I could no longer lift—behind. There was no salvation here on the earth. The most I could hope for was silence.

And I began to long for that final silence. In my longing, death did not look cold. Or sad. It looked languorous, that motionless end of everything here. Seductive, calling me. I tried it out on my husband, the only person I trusted with such a dark vision.

"I want you to know something about how I feel. It's important to me that you listen."

"Okay." He knew of my pain, but did not know what to do about it. Not being able to do anything was hard on him.

"What I have to tell you is that I want to be dead."

He said nothing. He waited.

"I want to stop and not have to start again." He still did not move or speak. This I didn't like. I wanted him to do something. I didn't know what it was, but I wanted it. Even now, I still do not know what it was that I wanted him to do.

"Listen, I'm not going to kill myself. I don't want you to think I might do that. I won't." This needed emphasizing. I was not suicidal: no hoarding of pills, no planning of my own execution, no "ideation." I would not kill myself. But I wanted to *be dead*. Wanted it to *happen* to me. I wanted to be taken out. Wanted it.

"When you're dead," I went on, "you don't have to do anything. You just lie in your box. You're in the ground with earthworms and seeds and other dead people, and you don't know or care. You don't mind. You are quiet." I paused, and then I added, "And your spirit finally knows what it is to be with God, with nothing in the way, and it's a wonderful thing to be with God." I was pretty sure that was the case. I thought about heaven a lot.

This was a hurtful thing to say to one who loved me deeply. That I wanted to die, that the sweetness of his presence was not sweet enough to make me want to live.

Duty, on the other hand, was *more than* enough to keep me alive. I had a duty to be alive. I had a duty to him, to my children and grandchildren, to my church. I am not a person who shirks duty. I would not shirk the duty of being alive.

But I didn't have to like it.

At night I lit more candles in crystal holders and eased myself into hot baths of lavender-scented water. The scent of the lavender rose with the steam; the heat of the water eased my aching joints. I took my old prayer book into the bath with me, my wet hands pocking the thin pages with marks of water drops. The ancient words of the Church's daily prayer rose from me, thick with tears. At other times, I took the same prayers to the chapel, where everything was clean and good, where the sun slanted through the stained glass and pooled rainbows on the floor. There, I often was not alone: another worshipper or two would join me, and the ancient words were a sweet conversation: "O God make speed to save us." "O Lord, make haste to help us." *How lovely this is,* I would think as we went back and forth. *How lovely,* as we sang the words antiphonally at Sunday vespers.

How lovely. The depressed often report a loss of the experience of beauty, a flatness that covers everything once held dear and colors it gray. That was not my experience: rarely in my life has the beauty of prayer, of art, of music, of *everything* been more vivid to me than during those painful days. And rarely have I been so unable to derive anything from it beyond the ache of my own isolation. It was as if I beheld intense beauty through an impenetrable window of thick glass. I could not tear myself away from the loveliness, but neither could I become lovely.

The tomb of my misery barricaded itself against the persistent rapping of my anger at its door. *No, I am not angry.* Sorrow was august. Anger was unacceptable. But a tic-like drumming of my clenched hand against my right thigh when someone irritated me became more and more frequent. "Stop that!" my daughter ordered when she saw me. "Do you know how you look when you do that? If you're mad, just say so." Mad? *Moi?* My anger was silent, or so I thought. In reality, it was getting louder: my voice more clipped, my tolerance of small inconveniences more slim, my strange beating of myself more obvious to others, more self-mutilating than before. It cannot have been a comfortable thing to see.

I will get up and take a walk in the morning, I promised myself each night. The endorphins generated by walking will help me feel better. Then I will have some energy. But my eyes flew open at ungodly hours—two, three. I would creep from our bed and take up residence in the guest room, tuning the radio to the BBC. Only the Brits and I were up at that hour. I would lie there in the scented dark—more candles—and listen to the cricket scores until I fell asleep. And then, at the normal waking time, I could not arise until it was time to go to work. I worked all day, every day. I worked from early morning until late at night. I worked and slept and woke up to listen to the cricket scores and sleep again, fitfully. And then I arose and went back to work.

It seemed necessary, all this working. Necessary, but it seemed also to do little good.

My desk was covered with ineffectual piles of unmet obligations; one was dispatched only at the expense of another, and none were ever satisfied. I gave hurried lip service to healthy-minded ideas about what the clergy should do: they should take time for themselves, they should have a life outside the parish, they should get enough rest, they should take a sabbatical. But the "shoulds" in each of these unexceptionable recommendations rang in my ears louder than anything else, drowning out any grace they might have offered. All of their gentle counsels took their places among the mountain of my unmet obligations. They felt no different from any of the others. Beyond the feeble palliation of stolen massages and scented baths and candles in crystal holders, my behavior gave not the slightest indication that I understood anything at all about self-care.

Oddly, so oddly that it can only have been by the grace of a loving God—who must by now have regarded me and those entrusted to my care with alarm—my desperate condition ordinarily did not get in the way of my doing many people genuine good. From somewhere in its depths I daily summoned reserves of empathy and patience beyond what made any sense at all. I managed to preach with power. Looking back, I recall now that many of my sermons were about dying and going to heaven. Too many. And they were too heartfelt. That, and the surreptitious beatings I endured at my own hand, would have been signs of my distress to anyone who knew the code. But few people did. And I certainly wasn't talking.

We will be true to Thee 'til death, we all sang one summer Sunday morning at the end of the 9:30 service. Another hymn about martyrdom, a favorite of mine. Something was strange, though: the room seemed to be concentrated in a tunnel ringed with black. Everything seemed to have slowed down. I sank to the floor at the chapel steps. *I'll just rest.* For how long? A minute? A year? Eventually, I awakened, covered with my own vomit and surrounded by a circle of frightened faces, protesting only weakly when the emergency medical services came to cart me away and not at all when a cardiologist who was suddenly *mine* cleaned out a blocked artery in my heart as casually as he would have unstopped a kitchen drainpipe.

Oh. *That's* what's wrong. I have a heart condition. Neat and clean, a heart condition—except for the vomit. Physical and, it later turned out, electrical as well. Arrhythmia. Medicines for it. Lots of medicines. Maybe a pacemaker. Electrical. Oh, good.

I would rest. I tried and failed to write—too tired. My pulse was in the thirties; no wonder I was tired. I read murder mysteries. I dozed through visitors. I slept all night and much of each day. I came home. I sat at the picnic table. It was beautiful and green in the garden. A heart condition. How lovely.

I was back at work in two weeks. The vestry made me promise to moderate my work schedule. *Yes, I will.* And I did. I kept a log of my working hours. I didn't count the telephone work from home, or the fourteen-hour Sundays. *Progress, not perfection,* I told myself. I told myself and others that I was slowing down. That was not true. I was speeding up, slowly.

When the World Trade Center collapsed, though, there was no pretending any more. All bets were off. Prayer vigils. Food collections— food, and clean socks and eye drops and stuffed animals, pouring into the church from all sides.

We were in New York, and we could get these things to the site, couldn't we? Yes, certainly. Tragedy brings out the best in people, but it also brings out the worst: the drunks got drunker, the crazy got crazier, the needy got needier. All around me, people were either rising magnificently to the occasion or falling apart. Some were doing both.

Interestingly, *I* felt better. Of course I can help. Of course I have time to talk. Of course I will go. Who could stay away? The pile of twisted metal and plastic and paper and dust and hidden bits of human flesh and bone rose high above the ground and went down many stories below it. Workers swarmed over it like ants. The train stations and construction fences were papered with color photocopies of the missing: *Maybe she became confused and wandered off, and at this very minute maybe she is somewhere in this city, huddled with other amnesiac WTC office workers around a rusty trash can with a fire burning in it to keep them all warm. Maybe.* Maybe. Because you can't disprove the negative, can you?

This was terrible. It was so terrible my own darkness became irrelevant, a grandiose bid for neurotic attention. *Don't you know what's happened here? How can you think about your own despair at a time like this?* And I didn't. Not me. And—again by the grace of a loving God who sighed and used even me—I and the people of God with whom I lived and worked put their shoulders into helping, all of us, became part of the greatest outpouring of human kindness New York had seen in a long, long time. Maybe ever.

My adversary just waited. It knew that I was no match for it, that it didn't matter how important my important work was. It knew its patience would be rewarded, but I did not know. I thought I was better. It was good to feel effective again. Good to know there were concrete, exhausting tasks on which to spend myself. Good to lead. Good to be good. Vestry records from those months show that I reported that I was completely healed, that I had never felt such a sense of purpose, that I was my old self now. The drug of care for others coursed through my veins. I see now that it was a hallucinogen. It allowed me to believe that I was fine. I was not fine.

Because I could not allow myself to acknowledge my own hidden pain, my body once again did the honors. Another collapse: I began to stammer slightly during the announcements, saw the same tunneling blackness, allowed as to how I needed to sit down, looked without speaking at the same alarmed faces, and allowed myself to be led away.

Nobody was buying my lies now. I had not slowed down like I said I would. I had attempted

to bury my disease in the dry leaves of my frantic
performance, in the embroidery of my duties. More
heart medicine. More reassuringly technical scans
and tests. And something else, now: medicine that
would insinuate itself into the chemistry of my
brain, that would tamper with my own way of
interpreting what happened in my world. The
juice of joy was in short supply among the neu-
rons; the medicine would help me make more.
Imagine.

The heart thing was real. I had a real blocked
artery. The arrhythmia was real, too. Dangerous
things, both of them. But I know that the real reason I could not continue was the crushing weight
of unacknowledged despair that I carried with me
everywhere. I believe that my body's wisdom tri-
umphed over my mind's denial so that I could live,
and I believe that I would have died if my body
had not given out and given up. I never would
have killed myself, but I would have seen to it that
the church killed me. Had it been left to me, I
never would have stopped. And I would be dead
now.

And I am not dead. I am alive. My life has
changed dramatically. I have said good-bye to
people and things I hated to leave, chief among
them my brave, funny little church and all the
beloved people in it. I have told the truth about

what I can and cannot give. Sparingly, I have even told it out loud, in public, and have been rewarded for that judicious sharing by the answering stories of many other good and faithful people who have battled my old enemy, too. *Do you have a history of depression?* one of them will ask, seeming a bit surprised that I would own up to such a thing in front of people, and I answer with a firm *Yes*. That *Yes* may be the greatest gift I have left to give.

We're Not Climbing Jacob's Ladder

I *would just be worried about your career,* my friend said, genuinely concerned. *I mean, where would you go from there?*

I knew that he meant "where would I go that would be in an appropriately upward direction." He was talking about a position in which I was interested. I was thirty-one years old and just thinking about what might be next. The thing that would ordinarily be next for a young priest just finishing her first curacy—this was at a time when there weren't many *hers,* of any age, finishing any curacies, so it was a great honor to have a position at all—would be a small parish of her own and then a larger one until it was time to accept a call to a really large and wealthy one. There was clearly a ladder of success in the Church, and the rungs were clearly marked.

The position I was looking at was that of chaplain on the waterfront. That wasn't even a rung. On the waterfront? *That's a bad idea*, another friend said. *You'll disappear there. Nobody will ever hear of you again. You need to keep up your visibility. You've got to think of the position* after *the position you take.*

I do?

The position *after* the position I take?

That's the advice anyone might give anyone else in any profession. Somehow, though, it did not smell right to me in the context of priesthood. Is it really true of priests that they should always be looking down the line to the next plummy job? Are priests really supposed to be that strategic? Is it just a job, like any other job?

For that matter, is it really true of anyone? Should *anyone* be that strategic? Shouldn't I seek to be in the place in which I am using my gifts to the best of my ability *right now*, interested and interesting, curious and eager to learn and do right now—rather than peering down the tracks to see when the next train's coming?

"Portraits of Grief" was the title of the *New York Times'* capsule obituaries of all those who

perished in the 9/11 disasters. So many people—
in the buildings, but also in the planes. People who
were at the top of their game and people just
starting out. People who ordinarily wouldn't have
been there that day at all. People who had always
wanted to work in the World Trade Center or the
Pentagon and finally did. People who were count-
ing the days until retirement. People who traded
bonds during the day and sang opera at night.
People about to get married. People about to have
babies. The job to which they went on the eleventh
of September was the last job they ever had.

There may be such a thing as being too strategic. Our hold on today is tenuous enough that
we'd all better be sure we really love it, really live it,
really consider it. Before it's gone.

I took the waterfront job.

My friend was right: I experienced an immedi-
ate loss of status. Nobody in the Church really
knew what I did for a living. I was as marginal in
the ecclesiastical world as the people I served were
in the world of work. Nobody on the waterfront
was there to go to church. They were there to do
their jobs. The chapel was parenthetical. Many
times I offered a Mass and nobody came.

Marginal. Except when a young man died on
board a Swedish ship and his captain had to tell
his parents it was from alcohol poisoning.

Or when the *Lloyd Bermuda* went down in a storm, with all hands.

Or when a man ended up in jail and his ship had to leave without him.

Or when another man was injured and the owner wouldn't take him to the hospital.

Or when two stowaways were run over by a truck on Corbin Street.

Or when a man's mother died. Or a far-away woman's husband. And a trucker's little boy.

Or when somebody got shot in the kneecap during a strike. Just one guy. That's all it took. Nobody else crossed the picket line after that.

You don't become a bishop by working on the waterfront. But you do become part of the world of work, that world by which most people define themselves as human beings. You do bring the body of Christ into the world to which Christ came and for which Christ died. You are part of its ambiguous dying and rising, again and again. You learn that "the poor" makes a lousy group noun. That people from the same part of the world don't "all look alike." You learn that there is no such thing as menial work.

It could get cold there, down by the water. That was before we renovated the Seafarers' Center. There were week-long stretches with no heat, when we would go out in the van to search for abandoned wooden pallets and burn them in the Center's fireplace to stay warm. The doors to the Center would freeze shut, and I'd have to use my cigarette lighter to get them open. The ships were warm inside, though, as long as the engine was running. Your feet would tap along the metal deck in the cold and dark and you opened the accommodations door and there would be the bright lights in the shabby corridors, the crew drinking coffee in their lounge, the cook making soup, the captain on the phone.

Before I knew it, seven years had passed. I had not "disappeared." I continued to be all the things I had been when I went to the waterfront, and became a few other things besides. I was older now. I had worked at something I never would have encountered and discovered a love for the sea and those who sail it that will never leave me.

I now believe that the ladder of success is irrelevant to anyone who seeks a meaningful life. Some of us will be rich and some of us will be poor and most of us will struggle along somewhere in the middle. Some of our names will be household words and most will not. The notion of "call," a word used often in church circles and hardly at all anywhere else, is a word that needs more play. We all have a destiny, but our destiny is not located at the end of a rainbow or the top of a ladder. Our destiny is to make the present count. It could be the only future we have. If my place right now is not a place of interest to me, I will shrink, not grow. God doesn't usually annihilate our interests and desires in order to carry us to our destinies. Our desires are part of our destinies.

From the waterfront, I went to a very wealthy church. A church at the very top of the ladder. A church that probably owned the ladder. Life there was both profoundly enabled and profoundly disabled by its great wealth. There was little in the way of resources we did not have. It was hard to believe that I made much difference in the midst of all that richness, though. I found myself longing for the street.

St. Clement's was on the street, all right. The office at St. Clement's was where used office machinery went to die. None of the chairs matched. Many windows were broken, and the wind whistled in around the same packing tape with which they had been mended twenty years ago. Another *non sequitur,* in terms of climbing the ladder of success, but I was utterly at home in *non sequiturs* by now and had come to prefer them.

Here is what I think: the hardest, poorest places should have the best people. But they usually can't get them, because those folks are snapped up by rich places, and before long they can't afford to work anywhere but in a gilded cage. This is a pity. It uncritically endorses the world's questionable equation of money and power with worth, and passes it along to people preparing for ministry.

This was the philosophy that took me to St. Clement's. As a careful reader will have already noticed, it did presuppose that I was *among* those best, those worthies who should go to hard places and transform them. This had never been proven. It presupposed that I would be able to cope and even triumph over St. Clement's many obstacles.

You transformed the place, people told me when I left. Did I? Many things were better than when I came there. Some weren't. We didn't do everything we wanted to do. I didn't stay as long as I wanted to stay, but I stayed as long as I could.

Transformed? I still don't know. I know it transformed me. But I was still recognizable as myself. And St. Clement's was still St. Clement's.

This Thanksgiving, for the first time in I don't know when, I did not have a community dinner for two hundred people to shop for, plan, or help prepare. St. Clement's was famous for its community dinners. I thought of them as the piles of turkeys began to appear in the frozen food section of the supermarket. Will they do the dinner this year? Will they be all right without me?

I did not call and ask. I heard from somebody that Rebecca Scott was in charge of it, and then Brad Lewis sent me a flyer announcing it. Good signs. Then I happened to be over at St. Bart's, and ran into J. D. Clarke. Well, actually, I *asked* to see him, so that I could remind him that they always give us turkeys to cook, and that maybe he should call and offer. He looked at me a little strangely and smiled, and then he said they'd already taken care of that, that Deacon Geri Swanson had asked him for turkeys weeks ago. *Don't worry about them, Mama*, he said.

The dinner was great, Rebecca's mom told me. I had just happened to mention it when I called her to see how she was feeling these days. *Oh, it was fine*, she said, *they did a beautiful job.*

God transforms things. We just show up and do our best. The fate of an institution probably doesn't hinge on whether we go there or not. We'll do as well as we can wherever we are. In the end, we'll want to have been fully awake and fully engaged wherever we found ourselves. So get there now, wherever it is. Be present to the actual doing of your work now, for its own sake, not for the sake of some work you might have in the someday future. Someday may be right now.

Wedding Day

❧

We went to Elkton.

I don't know that many people today know about Elkton. They would have no reason to know. But readers of a certain age will remember a long period in the last century when Elkton, Maryland, was a marriage mill—like Las Vegas, but no Wayne Newton.

I wore a bright yellow suit that was too old for me. It was a suit my mother would have worn— mid-knee, in *1968,* for heaven's sake. I wanted to look as old as I could. I was ashamed of my youth, in view of what I was about to do. What I *had* done, I mean. Somehow, I thought, the disgrace would have been less if I had been older.

But I was only sixteen.

I remembered a woman I had known as a child. She had been married at thirteen. I had always wondered what it was like to be her, married to a much older man, a man in his thirties, mother to five or six children by her early twenties. She seemed always to be washing clothes. She was from the mountains down south somewhere, where such a thing was not unusual. There were still many states in which the age of consent for a girl was fourteen.

Juliet Capulet was thirteen. I remembered that. I do not believe the woman from the mountains down south knew about Juliet Capulet. They did not know each other.

But I knew Juliet. She was my first Shakespeare, if you don't count sonnets. I knew about Juliet, and about Hamlet, and a few things about electrons. I knew who Robespierre was. I could recite the Periodic Table of the Elements, as it then stood: I believe they have since added some new ones, although I am not sure. I had proved the Pythagorean Theorem and memorized the kings and queens of England in order of their appearance. I had won a prize in French; I got a certificate that read *Prix d'Honneur*. I had gone all the way to Baltimore to compete for my *Prix d'Honneur*.

Elkton was some distance from Baltimore. About fifty miles in the other direction. In terms of *honneur*, it was even farther. My parents followed us there in their car—only my parents, as his did not attend. I am not sure they were invited.

We found a minister, whose precise denominational affiliation was unknown to us. The four of us stood awkwardly before him in his living room, listening with half our minds while he paid a few compliments to commitment and religion in marriage, took the vows, blessed the rings, pronounced the marriage. A hurried kiss between the bride and groom; another, I think, between my mother and me. I could feel the rage and sorrow in her embrace. The minister beamed improbably. I do not now remember whether my new husband paid him or my father. My husband was probably too young even to know that you paid the minister. My father shook my husband's hand. That must have cost him dearly. I think I knew that at the time.

We drove off. The two of us drove to Baltimore. We saw a movie whose title I do not now remember and went to a restaurant my mother liked a lot. I really didn't know any other restaurants in Baltimore. If you had told me that my frumpy attire, the restaurant, my desire to cook and clean for this bewildered young man were all about cutting myself loose from my mother and

then striving to resemble her, I would have said
you were quite mistaken. On the car radio going
home, they played a stupid song: "I Just Dropped
in to See What Condition Your Condition Was
In." My parents' wedding song had been "Always."
I wondered if I had stumbled into an alternative
universe of inappropriateness. *This is my wedding
night,* I thought as we drove. *What the hell kind
of wedding song is this?* I quickly repressed the
thought, and he seemed unaware that people even
had wedding songs. I don't believe he had ever
been to a wedding.

Could the evening have been sadder? Yes, I
suppose it could have: we could have died. But I
didn't know it was sad at the time. I was resolutely
cheerful, and told myself that we would smile in
remembrance of it years from then, when we were
prosperous and grownup and comfortable and
ecstatically happy. Like my parents.

They were heartsick, my parents. I managed
both to know that and not to know it at the same
time. I was too young and uninformed to be heartsick. I was still magical, all but immortal. Many of
life's rules still didn't apply to me—most of them,
in fact—and I was still able to believe many things
that were manifestly untrue. I was aware of my
shame, but it would not last. My shame would be
temporary: I would prove myself. I was beginning

a life that could be anything I chose to make it. I had an exaggerated confidence in my range of options. I would reinvent myself. But there were questions I did not ask myself, not with any honesty: How would we live, and where, and upon what? How would I continue my schooling? With what? And who would this little life inside me turn out to be? What about *that?* The baby I carried was so tiny and new that the only decision I had made for her so far was the decision to let her live. I had no sense of her as a person separate from me; how was it that she would become one? The questions nibbled at the edges of my mind, but I allowed them no further entry. I was still magical enough to discount the obvious limitations of the life I was to enter.

My sister-in-law gave us an after-the-fact wedding party in their tiny apartment. A cake, and nice food. She always did things so nicely. She could put a party together with a jar of mayonnaise and two placemats. I would be like her, I thought, competent like that, a wonderful hostess and homemaker. I could feel the compassion for me in the little party, and could not resent it from her: she was young, too, like me, and had put herself on hold, too, like me. It was a lovely party. I suppose Karl Marx would have said we were putting garlands on the chains. I had not yet read Karl Marx.

I had also not yet read Betty Friedan. That was coming.

Statistics are against you, my middle brother said, unkindly. I was hurt by this, although part of me knew it was true. Girls who had to get married didn't usually continue their educations. But I was angry. My brother did not seem to understand how special I was. How different. He did not seem to understand that if you wanted something badly enough, it happened.

The Power of Positive Wanting. Lord, have mercy.

Besides, it was not *my* education I was concerned about. It was my husband's. When asked how I was, I would answer with a statement about how *he* was. I was ridiculously eager to support his education, his life, to bear his child, to cook his meals and wash his clothes. I won a scholarship and went to ask if I could apply it to *his* tuition. The administrator of the scholarship was nonplussed. I think now that I was afraid of my own life and wanted to borrow his.

In no way was he ready to be a husband, let alone a father. As the months of our brief union continued—less than three years in all—and the reality of what this life meant and what it contained, of who he really was and the persistent memory of who I really was, as these things became

clear as things only become clear when they are
lived, I grew less and less willing to immolate
myself upon the pyre of his life. My brother's pre-
diction turned out to be a good thing, a great favor
to me: dire predictions always steel my resolve to
prove them false. I expanded my vision to re-
include myself. My embrace of my own autonomy
was bumptious and self-absorbed, and it hurt my
husband. He became more and more depressed,
angrier and angrier. We shared less and less. Eventually, we shared nothing at all.

I wish now that I had had the courage to go it
alone and never involve him. I remember asking
him if that's what he wanted me to do. I must have
signaled to him in a dozen ways how he was supposed to answer: *No*, he said. That was probably
not a lie at the time. But we cannot always do
what we think we can do. I have judged myself
harshly in this matter for many years. Interestingly,
I have not judged *him* harshly. It was always easier
to forgive his immaturity than to acknowledge my
own. I continued to be afraid, afraid and ashamed
of my youth at that moment in my life, long after I
was no longer young. I was tainted for decades. It
is only lately, when my own children have passed
through young adulthood, when my *grandchildren*,
for heaven's sake, are approaching it, that I finally
have understood how young we were. It is only

lately that I have forgiven that young girl who was
too proud to admit that she was scared of her life.

I think, sometimes, about the woman I knew
who married when she was thirteen and stuck it
out all those years. Couldn't I have done the same?
Couldn't I have found a way? Couldn't I have
developed myself, my hobbies and my sewing and
my reading, couldn't I have made a pearl around a
difficult husband, as so many women have done
for so many thousand of years?

Years later, he came to my brother's funeral.
They had been friends when we were all young. I
didn't recognize the portly, middle-aged man who
came toward me with a nervous smile: my greeting
of him by name was a product of deduction, not
recognition. That must be he. Who else would it
be? Did I really daydream about that face once,
love that body once?

I did, once upon a time.

Now his carriage was oddly stiff, as if his back
were fused with a metal bar. I must remember to
ask my daughter if he has had back surgery or
something. He was so tense, so nervous, so
avoidant of my eyes. Was he like that with everyone? Or just with me?

It was good of you to come, I said. And it was.
He said he was sorry about my brother. *Thank you.
Thank you for coming. Good-bye,* I said. *Good-bye.*

Q's Tower of Coffee

❀

"**W**ant some tea before we get started?" I ask Pam, who has just arrived for her monthly spiritual direction appointment. We've been together for years; I know she takes hers plain. Me, I like the carcinogenic sugar substitutes. Sometimes I can find a cookie or two to enliven the late morning, but mostly I can't and it's just tea. As I raise a modest clatter with cups and teapot, I see Pam notice something odd on top of the stove. It is a large-ish saucepan with about three inches of water in it. Our white ceramic coffee pot stands in the water. Atop the pot is its white ceramic filter holder, containing a paper filter filled with a few days' worth of sodden coffee. A saucer sits on the filter holder, and upon that is a coffee mug topped by another saucer, this one inverted. The whole ensemble stands about seventeen inches high.

"What on earth is that?" she asks.

"Well," I say, "Q has a special system for keeping his coffee warm."

"Why not just get an automatic coffee maker, like Mr. Coffee?"

Why, indeed? It would be impossible to explain, so I never do. *Here, take this home,* someone says, *you can heat it up in the microwave.* I never tell her we don't have a microwave. I know they're impossible to live without, but we've been doing without one for years. We heat things in a double boiler.

"I haven't seen your red sweater for a while," I tell Q one night. I have begged him to get rid of it for years; it is a tissue of holes. But Q loves his old sweater. Where is it?

"I buried it in the garden," he says comfortably, looking up from his book. I can't believe this. I've tried and failed to peel it off of him for so long, and he went and planted it?

"In the compost?"

"No, just in the garden. Birds can use the threads to make their nests." I shake my head in wonder.

Next time I'm outside, I survey the garden. There is the sweater, in effigy by now, south of

the tomatoes and right beside the stalks of last
summer's basil. It is a sight of no small pathos,
and I am cut to the quick by my own coldness
of heart. Now I've killed it. How could I have
been so unfeeling? But bits of red wool protrude
from the ground here and there. Sure enough,
birds have been helping themselves to the yarn.
Now every bird in town has a nest with red
accents.

"I can't believe you actually let that sweater go,"
I tell him when I come back inside. What I also
can't believe is that he said nothing about it. But
then I think again: this silence is of a piece with
the man I know. Q often communicates with great
eloquence by saying nothing at all. Putting away
some socks one day, I noticed two cans of tuna in
his sock drawer. That was odd. What were they
doing there? I asked him. "People keep taking my
tuna packed in water and eating it," he said. "And
then when I need it, I don't have any."

This seemed small. Could there not have been
some negotiation? I countered in the only way I
could: I put a muffin in his shaving dish. *Take that.*
But answer came there none—the muffin disappeared, but no words about it were ever exchanged.
I cannot now remember whether the muffin in the
soap dish did the trick with the tuna in the sock
drawer or not. I am sorely tempted to say that I

was never troubled by it again, but there is always the chance that he may read this.

I can't even think of getting a Mr. Coffee. Q's disgust was palpable when he learned that the company that makes Mr. Coffee had come out with a product called "Mrs. Tea." "Mrs. Tea!" As if brewing a pot of tea were a difficult task. Q is more incensed at capitalism's invent-a-need marketing than anyone I've ever known. Gas grills, automatic garage door openers, snow blowers: no, no, and no. Not just *no–I–don't–want–one* no, but *over–my–dead–body* no. Some battles are just not worth fighting.

He fetches me from the train station on a cold night. The twin seats in front are toasty warm, his and mine. They have heaters in them. He never would have ordered heated seats—they just came with the car when we bought it. But oh! how nice they are on a cold night or a frigid morning. I sink into mine with a sigh of luxury. Even he admits they are wonderful. As we pull away from the curb, I catch movement out of the corner of my eye. Someone is in the back seat. I turn around and see one of the cats. She is standing on her hind legs and looking nonchalantly out the window.

"You've brought a cat."

"She wanted to go for a ride," he says, signaling for a left turn. The cat almost loses her footing, but quickly regains her poise and continues to gaze out the car window.

"Cats don't go for rides."

"This one does. She wanted to feel the wind in her face."

Cats hate wind. "Why do you think that?"

"She told me." He imitates the cat, who often *does* utter long strings of syllables that seem intended to transmit thought. So maybe she did tell him. This isn't the first time he's brought a cat along when he picks me up. He doesn't know that cats don't go for rides. Now they seem not to know, either.

"Picnic" has become the technical term for a meal eaten in front of the fire because the dining table is covered with papers that cannot be moved. Our little coffee table barely holds our dinner plates; we have to set the wine bottle on the floor. We picnic a lot, he and I. Last night it was pizza, which really has to come to the table in its pan so you can keep the pieces warm. Where to put the pizza pan? I saw that another Q tower had sprung up in the course of the day over by his reading chair. It consisted of the two-volume *Oxford English Dictionary* set horizontally atop its strong cardboard case. That'll do just fine, I thought. I put a placemat on Volume I, and dinner was served.

It comes of having been a Scout, I think, the way he jury-rigs through life. There is a quiet exhilaration to be had in appropriating an object to a purpose not its own, the pleasant, resourceful feeling of being able to make do in any situation. Its attraction grows with age: I, too, am not as interested in every gadget that comes along as I once was. I, too, find myself liking the same old clothes, resisting new ones. "You're getting to be like Q," my children warn darkly. I know.

"You're not going to get serious about him, are you, Mom?" Anna asked upon meeting him for the first time. She was about ten. He was fifty-seven. He wore a beret and, frequently, an ascot. I don't believe she had ever seen anyone in an ascot; Q was Anna's first ascot. He also wore Space Shoes, special handmade-just-for-Q footwear that were supremely comfortable but made him look like Mickey Mouse from the ankles down. His tweed jackets were fraying badly; a corduroy one was in better shape, but was an unusual persimmon color. All of his jackets were older than Anna; I suspected that one or two might be older than I was. His woolen scarf had belonged to his father, who had been dead for many years and had worn it for many years himself before he died. Never had my family seen so many antique clothes on a person who was still alive.

"Oh, no," I reassured her, "We're just friends."

But he was so *nice*. So direct and truthful. So enthusiastic about things, and so unembarrassed about showing it. So interested in people and, soon, so unmistakably interested in me. Seriousness was imminent. Anna would just have to get used to him.

Citizen Q has applied to be part of a long-term study to see if vitamin E and selenium prevent prostate cancer. Participants must be fifty-five or older, and must never have had prostate cancer. He was excited when he learned of it, and ran off photocopies of the invitation to join the study so he could distribute them to other men in his age group. He sometimes refers to himself, charmingly, as "a ruin." *I'll see if any of the other ruins want to do this.* Two other ruins are interested.

Q is always donating his body to science. He is part of another long-term study, this one following close relatives of Alzheimer's' victims; his mother died of it. He is a joyous donor of blood, having shed many gallons over the years. Real sorrow descended upon him when he was banned from donating for an entire year after a trip to India: the bombing of the World Trade Center occurred during that year, and he was unable to give blood.

"I'm the universal donor, you know," he said wistfully: O positive, the blood type compatible with more types than any other. People flocked to hospitals and blood centers to donate on the day of the bombing, camping out in front of them into the night and through the next day. But the need for blood was pitiably small: almost everyone who might have received it was already dead. Soon the shelf life of the blood that was collected passed, and most of it had to be discarded. By then, Q's year of exile was up, and he went happily to the blood center to help out with in the annual winter blood shortage.

I can't give blood. I take too many medicines, and I can't stay off them long enough to render my over-medicated blood presentable. My back hurts, so I can't run. I can only walk fast. Q breaks into a full gallop, though, when we get off the train, and makes it to the taxi stand ahead of all the other commuters. I lope along behind, and ease myself carefully into the back seat. He leaps in beside me. Q is twenty-three years my senior.

I used to be sure that I would be a widow. I was glad of it: I would be able to care for him when he got frail. Now I'm not so sure. He bounds around my friend's yard, imagining trees and plants in different spots on the blank canvas of wood chips that covers the empty ground. "Q is amazing," she says as we watch him from the car. He rarely walks. We rarely move. "How does he do it, I wonder."

I often ask myself that. He eats a banana a day.
Maybe that's it. He doesn't eat processed food.
That probably helps. Maybe it's the selenium. Maybe. But I have come to think that Q's secret of
eternal youth is approaching life as if he were a
child. Children see the oddities of life, the curves
and straightness of things, the varieties in colors,
the breaks in meter: all to which we have become
accustomed are new to them. And Q sees things
freshly like that, like children do. He lacks the
ennui gene.

I squeeze out a kitchen sponge and lay it flat on
the counter. He takes it and sets it on its edge
among the plants in the little bay window over the
sink. "It'll humidify the plants," he says, "with
more of its surface exposed to the air." Good grief.
But now I, too, set the sponges on their edges. It
can't hurt.

I brought my geraniums in for the winter to
live in this window, where they would have sun
and bloom. In one of the geranium pots an uninvited tomato plant sprouted, born of a composted
tomato. Well, I never. I was all for pulling it up,
but Farmer Q would have none of it. "It's a *volunteer*," he protested, and I paused. Fatally. Oh, a
volunteer, like a hospital volunteer or a literacy volunteer or a volunteer at the World Trade Center
site. Oh, dear. I couldn't pull up a *volunteer*.

I breathed a few threats about what might happen if the tomato shaded my geraniums, who were *there first*, preventing them from blooming. I told him that the tomato vine would just grow long and leggy and ugly and that it would not produce tomatoes in any case in the winter in a window in New Jersey, for heaven's sake. I said it would be a miracle if we had a tomato from this vine in the winter, one I would interpret as a sign that I needed to learn to be more flexible.

The thing grew. I was right; it was leggy. I had to move some of the geraniums to better windows, it took up so much sun. But then it produced a few flowers. Hmmn. And one day he directed my attention to a tiny tomato. Damn. As spring approached, the tomato grew. It grew to a diameter of about two inches. The vine nods insolently at me when I pass it going down the driveway on my morning walk. *Smart aleck.* But I give it grudging respect: it has claimed life from death, made the case for its survival based solely on its unlikely potential, and secured the advocacy of a man I now know to be a formidable foe, who understands that I am a sucker for bravery in others. And it has won.

"Are you old?" I ask Q one night, as he reads in his chair and I sit in mine watching him read. He looks up. "I guess so," he says.

"You must be." The numbers work. He was born during the Coolidge administration. "You just don't seem like I always thought a person ought to at your age."

"I never thought about it." He goes back to his book.

I will be more flexible. I will see the possibilities in those things that interrupt my plans. I will eat a banana a day. I will respect old clothes and old automobiles and old ways. And I will enjoy this old man—if that's what he is—while I still have him.

Carjacked

❧

The terse newspaper accounts did not name my husband. "A retired college professor," one called him, and another was even more dismissive: "a retiree." I had not, until that moment, thought of our carjacking in terms of elder abuse, but the paper made him sound ancient.

I was walking with other weary commuters toward the line of waiting spouses in warm cars, come to meet our train. I did see the young man in the front passenger seat as I approached, but he looked to me like a graduate student. One of my ancient husband's alumni, I figure, cadging a lift. But the body language was wrong when I got in: my usually gregarious spouse was silent and sitting very still. So was the young man in the ski cap.

"I just want to get to Newark. That's all I want, and I'll get out," he said tightly.

My husband explained that we weren't going to Newark, that we were going to Metuchen, but it did not seem to me that a dialogue was taking shape. The young man repeated his request. Suddenly I got it.

"Wait a minute!" I said loudly, and flung open the door. *"Get out of the car!"* I shouted to the young man as I leapt out. He looked at me blankly through the car window. I looked back. In his hand I saw a hypodermic syringe. It was filled with a red fluid. Holy God.

"This man has a hypodermic needle!" I yelled to several startled commuters. I yelled a few other things, too: Help me get the door open! Help me hold the car! Help me call 911! Just help me!

The young man pointed the syringe menacingly at my husband and fumbled with the steering wheel. I pulled fruitlessly at the locked door and shouted. Off they drove, I running behind them screaming. After a moment, I was alone on the ground level of the parking garage. I called 911 on my cell phone. The police came. We went to the station. For two hours nobody knew whether Q was alive or dead.

I got out and he didn't. I let a carjacker drive off with my husband. The syringe was enormous in my memory, sharp and poisonous and trained on the man I adore. "They do that," the detective said laconically. "Junkies. They fill a needle with red food coloring so you'll think it's blood." I think he was trying to make me feel better.

The carjacker would shove the needle into Q's arm and push the plunger. HIV virus by the millions would course through Q's bloodstream in seconds, and he would die. Or the man didn't have AIDS, but the needle was full of curare, and my husband would be rendered unable to move. Or it was full of air, and a bubble of air would travel to Q's brain and lodge there, and he would be unable to speak ever again. He would never again tell me the prologue to the *Canterbury Tales* in Middle English in bed. He would never again sing his Russian song in the shower, sounding like a bear. We would never argue again. What had already been said would turn out to be all there was to say.

Or the young man also had a gun that I hadn't seen, and my husband was already dead.

The house was full of cops when Q finally came home, life and car intact, not stuck with a needle but short a few hundred dollars, irritatingly calm and unafraid. He was peeved because they kept leaving doors open—"You're heating the outside!"—

and because he was intent on eating his dinner right away, trying to re-enter his routine as if he had never left it, rewinding the past few hours so they wouldn't have happened. The young officer saw this, and kindly desisted. "Come on down to the station when you're finished," he said.

By the time Q got to the police station, the detectives already had some thoughts on who the carjacker was. People on drugs don't plan ahead very well: two stops were made at two different cash machines, each of which hazily recorded the perpetrator's face on its surveillance camera. The second ATM was at a convenience store well known to cops and addicts as a heroin source. They had driven up to Newark, my husband talking quietly to the young man. In return, he got the kid's life story—the real and the fictitious, a jumble of pain and avoidance of responsibility. "Don't look back here," he said at one point, as he pulled down his waistband and injected himself in the abdomen. Then, his veins serenely full of heroin, the young man got out, after giving Q careful directions to Route 78.

When the police returned in a few days with a sheet of photographs, I was unable to identify our assailant. I hadn't seen much: a profile, the back of a neck, a scared white face looking up at me through a car window. Q, on the other hand, had spent two hours with the young man. "Don't look at me!" he said threateningly several times, and then presented Q with numerous chances to study him with as much care as could be exercised under the circumstances: at the ATM, in conversation, through the rearview mirror, at the bizarre handshake upon leaving. "That's him," Q said quietly, pointing to one in the row of young blond men. The cops exchanged satisfied glances; it was the man they had in custody, neatly ID'd by the ATM video and well known to the Newark police from too many previous encounters.

Jamie Toto was a local boy. Friends' children knew him. He had drugged his way through the high school until neither he nor the school could take it any more and then he dropped out. His dad worked at my husband's university in the maintenance department. His mom had split long ago. There was a grandmother somewhere in the mix. Q met all these people at the trial, or at what would have been the trial. Carjacking is a heavy ticket. So is assault with a deadly weapon and so is kidnapping. Everybody knew that Jamie wouldn't be back in circulation anytime soon. The judge accepted a prosecution-defense deal to roll Jamie's offenses together in one messy ball of grievance and sentence him to fifteen years, of which he can be expected to serve about four.

If you are the victim, you can speak at the sentencing phase of the perpetrator's trial. Here is the letter Q wrote to Jamie Toto and read aloud in court.

The paths of our lives, yours and mine, crossed last January by an extraordinary coincidence. We each just happened to be there, with the blooded hypodermic needle in your parcel, and you saw an easy shot.

That's one reason why I find it hard now to blame you. During the ninety minutes we were together then, a strange degree of mutual trust developed between us, which has amazed me since: I trusted you not to hurt me if I kept my car at your disposal and made no sudden moves. You seemed to trust me enough to talk with me as another real person, not a nervous victim who might fly off the handle. Whatever steadiness there was to all this, I'm grateful for it; my luck was not all bad, and that awareness inclines me to forgive you for the threatened danger, and the uncertainty and terror you put my wife through.

Halfway through your fifteen years you will reach the age at which my son was deprived of a good and promising life by another extraordinary coincidence— a collision at 4:30 A.M. with a drunk driver on an otherwise empty superhighway. That was fifteen years ago, and when I think of the life he has missed, even the lows as well as the highs, I mourn for what you are missing, too. That you are missing some good things in life on account of your wrong choices does not lessen my sadness at the waste.

Give yourself a break! Do what you can during your prison term to prepare yourself to enjoy those pleasures of life that are free to all of us, once you are free. Ross's death has focused for me just how free the best things in life are. As soon as you have paid back our society for holding its laws and custom so cheaply, of course I hope for you the kind of fun, beauty, and fulfillment in life that my son is missing. One path toward that fulfillment we talked about last January is the answer to addiction that a twelve-step program can supply. Hearing firsthand how other addicts pretty much like yourself have learned—have taught themselves—to make healthier choices would be the foundation of a fuller, richer life outside, after your sentence is done. But also, getting clean again will surely make your confinement more productive and easier to take. I hope most earnestly that such an opportunity—an active NA program—will be available to you soon and steadily, and that you'll take full advantage of it.

"Are you going to visit him?" I ask one day, as we drive by the police station.

"I'd like to," says Q, glancing into the rearview mirror.

I wonder if he really will. I wonder how Jamie is doing in prison. Is he working the twelve-step program Q implored him to enter? At age twenty, with long blond hair and blue eyes, he's probably queen of a very ugly prom by now. And when he gets out? When's he's absorbed more violence and more naked racism and more humiliation? I wish he could have gone to a rehab instead of to jail. But he's bombed out of quite a few rehabs already, and he has a sheet as long as his arm. Twenty is young to be as short on options as Jamie is.

Q says he knew Jamie wasn't going to hurt him. How? "He was an amateur," he says. "For instance, he grabbed the gear shift to put it into forward so I would have to drive off. But it wouldn't move, of course, because I didn't have the clutch engaged. He didn't know that. He'd never driven a stick shift."

In a different set of circumstances, Q could have taught him how to drive one.

Listening to the story, I had a vague sense that Jamie wished Q were his dad. He knows that Q lost a son a little older than Jamie is now. He thinks that he should have been the one who died, not golden Ross, who had the gift for being loved that Jamie cannot seem to muster, the education that Jamie did not pursue, the freedom from addiction that eludes Jamie.

When Q himself was twenty, he was in his next-to-last year of college. He had spent the previous summer driving across the country in a Model A Ford with two other guys to his fraternity's national convention in Denver, where they would unsuccessfully defend their chapter's decision to pledge an African-American. After that, their fraternity was ostracized by the national and became a local, but the boys earned the admiration of *Newsweek* and *Life,* who editorialized on the goodness of what they had tried to do.

Theirs was the class that welcomed back the returning veterans of World War II, who swarmed into colleges and universities across the country on the GI bill. It was half again as large as a normal class, and the returnees were different in many ways from Q and his contemporaries, just a few years younger. An innocence drops out of people who have been to war, drops right out of them and never returns. There they all were, the young men and their slightly older, more sober classmates, all readying themselves optimistically for a life they knew would have a purpose. They expected it to be so, and so it was.

Jamie's innocence dropped out of him, too, a while back. But its departure was not accompanied by the eager purpose of the young veterans who filled the college classrooms of the late 1940s. They had won, these young men of fifty years ago, and all Jamie's ever done is lose. He can't even drive a stick shift.

My dream is that those of us who are more or less on top of things will take one who isn't and love him, and that our love will unravel the knot that binds them so profoundly, preventing them from ever spreading their wings, from even knowing they *have* wings. My dream is of each of us, each in our own dining room, sitting down to dinner at our own table, each with one guest, a guest we invite to use our homes and our families as a place to heal. My dream is that people can catch health from each other, like a benign cold.

This is a crazy dream. A few times, Q and I have lived it, this dream of loving a wounded stranger back into productive human society. Sometimes it has worked—never as smoothly and inevitably as we might have hoped, but enough to help someone get from Point A to Point B, and sometimes to C. But there is a whole alphabet of rungs on the ladder that connects the abyss of a strangled history with sustainable life in the human family, and it must be admitted that life in that family is, itself, a mountain once you get there. I imagine Jamie at table with us in the evenings, learning what it is to eat a meal in peace with gratitude to God. An unlikely feast, this meal with Jamie Toto. But I can imagine it.

Somewhere the hodgepodge of my foolish dreams of human love conquering all is a taste of the Love that really will. Will Jamie ever get his act together and become a productive citizen? There is simply no way to know. The signs so far aren't good, but people have come from further behind than he is and made it. Is there a love we can supply that will make up for his terrible beginning? Probably not. But are human beings always limited to the things they themselves produce, the powers they themselves have?

No, we are not. Sometimes good things happen that are beyond our ability either to bring about or to predict. When we think about the power of God it is usually when the reverse happens, when something that started out wonderful goes horribly wrong. Then we're all over the God question, torturing ourselves unanswerably about the causes of things. But tragedy isn't the only thing we know about; we also know about miracle. Miracle is a thing that comes from nowhere and shows us God. Nothing is outside the scope of its activity. Like tragedy, it cannot be predicted. But, as we have known tragedy, we have also known miracle to happen.

It would take a miracle to bring Jamie Toto around, to grow him into the adult God intends him to be. Exactly a miracle. I think of this when I imagine Jamie made whole and our having something to do with it: God bringing great good out of great evil. Live long enough and you see more than enough of both of these. It makes no more sense to prepare for one than for the other, to steel yourself for trouble or to open yourself to blessing.

It is warm today; a cooling rain has just begun to fall. I know it gets hot in prison, and I wonder if the rain cools things down in there. Or maybe they don't feel it at all. I'm sure Jamie has attended some twelve-step meetings by now—nothing better to do—and wonder if they have come to be more to him than an hour of listening to other people talk. It's possible that right now, at this very minute, he is listening earnestly, perhaps speaking himself. It may not be likely, but it is possible.

Jamie is sorry for kidnapping my husband, I know. I think Jamie is sorry about a lot of things. He has a lot to be sorry about. I am sorry, too. His parents are sorry and his grandmother is also sorry. Sorry hasn't gotten him much of anywhere, but it is a beginning.

People all over the Internet prayed for Q's safe return when he was carjacked. Back he came, in record time, safe and sound. That felt to all who loved him like the end of the story, a happy ending. But the story isn't quite over yet. Another character in it is unaccounted for. State law requires that the court notify the victim when a convicted assailant is released. We'll know when Jamie gets out of jail. Into the merciful care of the God who wants better things for him and from him, we commend Jamie. And we wait for word.

Fear Not

❧

I remember an argument I had with my brother when we were little. It was about angels. We had a picture book of Bible stories. Maybe you did, too, when you were a child, and maybe you still see those illustrations with your mind's eye when you hear a certain passage of Scripture, as I still do all these years later. Our grandmother was reading to us from the book—the Christmas story. There were shepherds, excited Middle Eastern men in bathrobes and furry vests, surrounded by lambs. And there, against the starry night, was the angel, a lovely young woman in a long, long pale blue dress, with enormous feathery wings and rays of light surrounding her blonde head.

At least, *I* said it was a girl. That was what the argument was about. David insisted that angels were boys. "They are not," I said hotly. I had never heard of such a silly idea. "Look at her. Look at her hair. Boys don't have long hair like that."

"That one does," he said stubbornly, and took the book from my grandmother's hands. After a moment of furious page-turning, he handed it to me triumphantly. "See?" he said.

I was dumbfounded. There was another angel, implacably standing guard at the entrance to the garden of Eden, while Adam and Eve skulked miserably away. This angel had long blond hair, too, but he also carried an immense sword, as big as he was and, what was more, the sword was *on fire*. Who could understand such a thing? That luxuriant mane of blond curls and those mighty arms, that flaming sword? Such incontrovertible evidence of masculinity and femininity in one contradictory body was too much for me. I decided not to pursue the argument, and turned back to the Christmas page.

"... and the angel said unto them, 'Fear not, for behold, I bring you glad tidings of great joy, which shall be to all people,'" my grandmother read, and I interrupted her. "Why did she say 'Fear not?'"

"Because the shepherds were afraid."

"But why were they afraid of her?" I persisted.

"*Him*," said my brother, but I took no notice.

"*Why* were they afraid?"

"Well," my grandmother thought for a moment. "I guess they had never seen an angel before."

"But she's not scary," I persisted. "She's pretty."

"Well, they weren't expecting her, " my grandmother said, "Now, you two be quiet and listen." She continued the story.

And we were quiet, even though we were excited about Christmas and consequently had been tormenting each other for days because we just didn't know what else to do with ourselves. We let the old words wash over us—already familiar, even to us, although we were pretty new in the world. It was already an old story, even to little children, already a story that made us feel comfortable and secure, already a story full of the reassurance and safety for which everyone longs at this time of year. Already we had begun to do what Christians have been doing with this story for centuries: domesticating it, looking at it through the lens of our own need, rather than look at it on its own terms.

For it really is a story full of fear.

From the moment of the Annunciation to the Virgin Mary, who asked a logical question of her heavenly visitor—"How shall this be?" she asked, which is exactly what I would have said if that had been me—to the tense negotiations around the possibility of a divorce on grounds of infidelity, to the desperate search for suitable lodgings at the most vulnerable moment in a woman's life, the very moment of childbirth, the birth of Christ had from the outset been a very precarious thing. It was anything but smooth. Anything but reassuring. Not a thing about it suggested that this was going to be safe. It was dangerous in every way, a scary situation, one that required great faith in God on the part of all concerned.

Mary and Joseph, the way they looked in my Bible picture book: she so sweet and calm and young; he older, but also calm, strong, and dependable and reassuring—they are the Mary and Joseph we want them to have been, but they are probably not the Mary and Joseph who really were. The birth of Christ was, in its human dimension, a profound story about trust in God in the face of terrible adversity: marginal people in an occupied country coping with a difficult and uncertain situation. Only now, after it is over, do we see reassurance in it.

What they knew must have been fear.

Could the Blessed Mother have been afraid? Blessed Joseph? Jesus *himself*? When I find myself filled with fear, does that mean that my faith has abandoned me? Are fear and faith incompatible?

I don't see how that can be true. Fear and courage are certainly not incompatible: it takes no

courage at all to endure something of which one is
not afraid. A hero is one who stands firm even
though he *is* afraid, a person who accepts her fear
and goes ahead and does it anyway. Do we think
that Rosa Parks was not afraid when she refused
to yield her seat on the bus to a white man?
That Dietrich Bonhoeffer was not afraid when he
accepted martyrdom at the hands of the Nazis?
That Nelson Mandela was not afraid when he
faced down the edifice of apartheid. And we ourselves, when we face times of trouble and uncertainty and feel the chill of fear in our hearts, the
clutch of fear in our throats: does that fear mean
that we are not people of faith? Not at all—it just
means we have something pretty powerful to pray
about, right then and there. Fear is far from being
the opposite of faith. Fear is a powerful induce-
ment to faith. Frightened people are the ones who
know they really need some help.

I wonder what happened to that Bible picture
book. So many things from childhood are lost—
things we remember, pieces of furniture that seemed
always to have been there, and we thought always
would be. Where did it all go, all that hardware
that was such a part of our lives we barely noticed
it? I remember everything about the bedroom in
which we were reading that Bible story book: the
dresser and the photographs arranged on it, my

grandmother's hairbrush and hand mirror that matched, the chair, the curtains, the wallpaper. Now it is gone, and the house is gone, and my grandmother and my brother are gone. Where has it all gone, and so quickly? David and I didn't know then—although my grandmother certainly knew—how short life would be. It is very short, we all come to understand, and it is most fragile. You usually don't know this when you are little, but you come to understand it all too well. No wonder we are afraid.

Into this short, precarious life came the Son of God. Ultimate power poured itself into our powerlessness. The Creator accepted the frustrating, sad limits of the created. The source of life entered into a journey that would end in a death we all will face, each on our own particular cross. A group of simple men—and probably some women and children, too, for just about anybody could be a shepherd in those days—awoke on a hillside and stared, terrified, at visitors from another world with a message about this one. "Do not be afraid," was the message. "Tonight we begin the sanctification of all your sorrow, all your fear, every burden you bear. Tonight we begin a journey you can only begin in fear. But all your tomorrows will be lived in the palpable love of God."

All Flesh Is
As the Grass

Quitting

❧

T he air is crisp, finally, one of those autumn days for which New Yorkers pant through the endless heat of August. Out on the street, it's like Woodstock—people lounging on every space that could possibly serve as a seat, looking up at the blue sky, walking and talking along the sidewalk in twos and threes, brisk and laughing. They sit in sidewalk cafes and sip coffee today, not hiding in the air-conditioned dark restaurants like they did all summer. New fall clothes that have hung hopefully in the closets through weeks when it was just too hot to wear them emerged today along Fifth Avenue, some on the lithe young bodies for which they were designed and some on bodies like mine, which really should know better.

A city of smells as you walk along: a pizzeria, a bakery, a jackhammer sending up acrid clouds of dust, a beauty salon, the exhaust of a bus, the hot, clean smell of a Laundromat. And in front of each office building, each hospital, each store, a sharp, strong hit of tobacco smoke from a cluster of smokers standing near the door.

I do not inhale as I pass by. Years after I stopped smoking—fifteen? seventeen?—I still will not allow myself to savor the smell. I know that where my mind goes, my body will follow. Even now, in this essay, I will not discuss the times it catches me unawares, entering my nostrils before I can hold my breath or turn away. I don't want to talk about it.

About the times it smells terrible, I'll talk. About the way the stale smoke clings to hair and clothing just from being in a room where smoking has occurred hours before I even went there, I'll talk. About yellow teeth and muddy, thickened skin. About persistent coughs. About bags under my eyes. Sure: what would you like to know? But not about the sharp snap of a cigarette's smoke on a sunny fall day. I won't go there.

Both my parents smoked Chesterfields. In the car, after dinner, while ironing, while reading—all

the time. My father's first heart attack occurred
when he was fifty-four; my mother's congestive
heart failure began in her fifties. My brother
smoked Marlboros. He died when he was forty-
nine. My other brother was a Marlboro man, too.
He is fifty-nine, and very ill.

I am fifty-two.

My father stopped smoking abruptly when he
became ill, and lived another thirty years. My
mother tried, but after she died I found cigarettes
in pockets, in purses, cigarettes in the glove com-
partment of their car, packs of them in between
the sofa cushions. Not Chesterfields, but the newer
"light" cigarettes. *Better for you.* She was gone in
ten years.

My brother tried hard, and some of the time
he succeeded. He became diabetic in his mid-
thirties, and managed that condition beautifully.
But the smokes crept back into his life more than
once. He was alone in his apartment when he
died. His landlady came in when she saw he hadn't
picked up his newspaper. *Cardiomyopathy* is what
the death certificate said. His heart was twice its
proper size.

In the early days of my deliverance from cigarettes, I thought a lot about my heart and my lungs.
I used to imagine their tarry blackness, and the
patient work of the cells in dying and regenerating,

new each time, replacing the hardened old ones with soft, fresh new pink ones. I imagined their sincerity, their cheerful shoulder-to-the-wheel determination to win the war. Cell by cell, I was being cleaned. With every breath, I imagined myself growing pinker.

And I imagined what it would be like for them if I smoked again. For the cells in my lungs, on the walls of my arteries, for the cells in the muscles of my heart. It would be smashing a child's sand castle, throwing someone's newly frosted cake on the floor. On purpose. It would be throwing tomato juice on a freshly ironed white shirt, tracking in mud on a clean floor. It would be a cavalier dismissal of all their hard work.

It would be cruel. *I want all you cells to try and try to stay clean and strong. I want you to try hard and keep on trying, but I will sabotage your hard work every day.*

I thought often of the microscopic profundity of the cells' fidelity to me, of the fidelity of my heart, beating so many millions of times throughout all these years, growing from its tiny size within my mother's womb to its current adult dimensions. I thought of the cells of my lungs, desperately trying to stay clean for my sake, worrying about me. They were so loyal. I hadn't earned such loyalty. It was more than I deserved.

The jump start I needed was the Great American Smokeout. No extended period of planning preceded the plunge. I just heard about it on the radio the night before and thought I could probably manage a day. The next day I managed another one. And another. Seventeen years later, I'm still managing.

In these seventeen years, everything has changed. Doctors used to sell cigarettes on the television, in print, and on the radio. So did sexy, attractive women: ". . . *and*, they are mild!" one would coo suggestively, and teenage boys all across America wanted to take her home.

We used to smoke in meetings. We used to light each other's cigarettes while looking significantly into each other's eyes and blow smoke into each other's faces in romantic restaurants. We used to smoke in bed. We used to smoke in the car, carefully rolling down the window to flick our ashes outside onto the street because the ashtray was full. We used to smoke on trains and planes. We used to smoke in the bathroom at school.

Not me, actually. I didn't smoke in high school.

I smoked once in a while in college. I didn't go to college in the normal way, though. I never lived in a dorm. I didn't start school until I already had children. So some important opportunities to develop the addiction passed me by. I was in my mid-twenties when I began to smoke in earnest. The Surgeon General's report had been out for about ten years. Doctors had long since stopped selling cigarettes on the tube. I was way old enough to know better.

It didn't take long. I liked the fast-lane feel of smoking, the Hemingway-ness of its danger. What that was about, I don't know: I *hated* Hemingway. My smoking habit intensified when my mother died of causes clearly related to smoking. Why? I must have wanted to join her. Perhaps I thought I had *become* her. I quickly became as heavy a smoker as she had been.

Smoking represented an interesting and attractive contradiction to my priestly vocation, a contradiction of which I felt a curious need. Such a vice obscured the stern implications of my orders. I was *not* set apart. I was *not* holy. *I have to smoke,* I remember explaining to an incredulous friend who worried about me, telling her about my work as a maritime chaplain. *Everyone on the waterfront smokes, and I have to establish community with them.* Good Lord. My brand was called "More," long and skinny and brown and unusual-looking. *More.* It kind of went with the Hemingway thing.

When I chanted the canon of the Mass, the ends of lines cut off too soon: I couldn't sustain the breath. My singing was rough around the edges. I lost control over my break, that portion of a singer's voice where chest voice yields to head voice, where management of the breath is especially difficult and crucially important. There was less and less room inside my chest, less and less strong, flexible tissue that could expand steadily and contract with quick force.

I would have told you, by the way, that none of this was happening.

I would have summoned a deep breath and sung you a few notes from a comfortable place in my range, and they would have sounded full and good. I would have gotten to choose the notes, though. I would have pointed to my Herculean schedule as all the evidence anybody would need of my good health.

In the doctor's office, I felt smug as I got dressed behind the curtain. *No evidence of coronary artery disease,* a series of tests had concluded. Good. I was beating the rap. I slid into the chair in the doctor's office as he reviewed my chart.

No evidence of coronary artery disease, he said again. *Yet,* he added.

Yet? Yet? Well, *yet* wasn't *now.*

I tried to stop many times. Ten, maybe. And then the Smokeout helped me stop.

And seventeen years later I had a heart attack anyway. And an angioplasty. The anterior wall of

my heart is slightly thickened now. This is how it
begins.

Oh.

Did I stop too late for it to make a difference?
No, I don't think so. With my family history, I
wouldn't be sick by now if I hadn't quit. I'd be
dead.

If I knew I were going to die soon, would I
start smoking again because it wouldn't matter any
more? Would I? Will I?

Don't think I haven't thought of this.

No. No, I wouldn't. And I won't. Everybody
dies, and I have a fairly good idea of how it is that
I will die. Only an idea, though. I may not die of
congestive heart failure at all. I may get hit by a
bus, or a Steinway may fall on me when I'm
walking down the street in New York one afternoon. We may be in a war and I might die that
way. Or someone I'm trying to help might be really
crazy and kill me—that's probably the runner-up
to congestive heart failure, actually, in terms of
likelihood.

So I really don't know how I will die, and I certainly don't know when.

But I want to be free when I do. Clean and
free. I want to be able to smell and taste for as long
as I can smell and taste. I want to sing with power
for as long as I can sing. I want to have been as

good as I could be to the only body I will ever have. I want to have done everything I could do to stay around for as long as I could. I want to know I have set an example to children of life, not one that makes them court death. For years after I quit, my younger daughter used to dream that I was smoking again, and awaken in tears. Even today, all these years later, I hate knowing that.

I don't want to be Hemingway. I think the short choppy sentences for which he is so famous are monotonous. There. I've said it, and I'm glad.

Besides, Hemingway killed himself.

Love Among the Ice Picks

❧

I swear I didn't even *move.* I was just lying here asleep, minding my own business. Why would my knee begin to hurt? For no reason? The pain wakes me up, and soon I am awash in self-pity.

It feels like someone's sticking an ice pick into my knee, I complain to Q. People don't know what ice picks are anymore, maybe: they were long, pointed metal tools with a wooden handle, like an awl, which people probably don't know about anymore, either. You used them to chip smaller pieces from the large blocks of ice that were delivered to your door and put in the icebox. You used an ice pick when you wanted ice in a drink.

This is the thing about arthritis that I didn't realize until I had it: it's not just *activity* that makes it worse. It's also *inactivity*. Now what's *that* about? One or the other, please. But most patients have an especially bad time at night, and most patients are regularly awakened by pain. Makes no sense, but there it is.

You can get up and move around a bit, and it usually helps. Sometimes I pull the covers off the offending leg and lift it skyward, bending repeatedly at the knee, twenty or thirty times in the dark, hearing the scary crunch of bone on bone, feeling the strange splinted stiffness in a joint that used to be so flexible. It would scare a burglar in our room, if there ever were one: one long leg, rising with no warning from the silent bed, bending, flexing, bending, flexing, without a sound except the crunch. He'd be back out the window in no time.

I sleep again. An old woman in my dream asks me to show her my legs. I think she may be God, but she is also a dance teacher. *What happened to your legs?* she asks. *Show me.*

And I show her, like a child displays a skinned knee. *This one is from when the car hit me,* I say, showing her the faint scar from the contusion and the network of spidery blue veins below it, the swollen place in the ankle that never goes away. *And this one is the arthritis,* I say, showing her the lumpy knee. *I didn't hurt the knee,* I tell her, *just the hip above it. And it was ten years ago. But now the knee is bad on that side.*

She holds each leg in her hands and examines each one closely and kindly. *I know,* she says.

I used to be a dancer, I say. At the gym one day last week, I couldn't achieve my usual wide stretch on the abductor machine. Usual? *Former,* I guess. *I used to be a dancer,* I said to the machine. The machine didn't say anything.

I know you were, the old woman says, and strokes my knee once or twice. Kind.

She loves the misshapen ankle, the old scar, the painful joint.

Some things are fine. Others are gone. In yoga, my body is no longer able to stretch symmetrically. In the lotus position, my left knee goes right down to the floor, as it always has. The right one won't. And I can no longer tell if my knee is straight by how it feels. It's as if it were wrapped in duct tape.

Yoga is all about allowing your body to be a means of connecting to the peace and power of the universe. It is not about being the most limber student in the room—that competitiveness is something I bring to class, not something I find there. I am embarrassed, though, by my stiffness. I hadn't realized how important it was to me to be more flexible than other people. How important it is to be more *everything* than other people. How tiresome. I wonder idly if there is ever to be any end to my egocentrism. Probably not. The yoga teacher tells me to imagine myself bathed in soft white light. Good idea.

Today, the gym, for absolutely sure. No excuses. I've coasted along on having fallen down the stairs earlier in the week for entirely too long. It hasn't prevented me from doing anything else, so it shouldn't prevent me from working out. My minor injuries have nothing whatever to do with going to the gym or not going. That's my own little fraud.

I never cease to be amazed at my ability not to do things that are good for me—and not just good for me, but that I truly enjoy. I love the feeling I get when I exercise. I love playing on the equipment. I even love sweating. I love it all.

So why do I linger in bed instead of going to the gym? Why do I tell myself I'm not feeling well and stay away, when I know that going would make me feel better? Why do I whine that my leg hurts, when I know from long experience that going to the gym will make it hurt less? Why do I say I'm too tired, when I know that going to the gym gives me energy?

Well, I'm sure I don't know why, unless it's just that a body at rest tends to remain at rest. Mine is definitely a body at rest.

So today I will go there and spend an hour so and have a good time and emerge feeling wonderful. If my friend goes too, we'll solve the world's problems while we're there, but even if she doesn't, I will go and the world will just have to muddle along.

I have a friend who does Morning Prayer on the treadmill. Years and years of it have committed the recurring portions of it to his memory. He starts up the belt and starts walking: "Lord, open my lips." "And my mouth shall proclaim your praise." He goes on through the whole office, and then spends the rest of the time on the treadmill in intercessory prayer: for himself, for his friends and family, for his church, for everything, saving the appointed psalms and readings until he gets back home and can sit down and read them. The pounding of his feet on the moving rubber belt becomes music, the percussive *continuo* accompanying his prayer.

He's done this for a long time, so long that he has become conditioned to it. Now, when he jumps on the treadmill, it makes him want to pray.

Interesting: we can condition our spirits in the same way as we condition our bodies. At the same time, in fact. We can train ourselves to pray, to fall into prayer as we fall into a familiar step. We can imprint our prayer lives right on our muscle memory.

I wonder if I've lost strength in the week I've been away. Probably a little. But the inborn direction of the human body is toward growth and strengthening: give it half a chance, and it makes up for lost time with alacrity.

And for the spirit, the same. I pound along on the treadmill and think of a sermon: *Has it been too long since you prayed? Are you reluctant to start again, embarrassed by your long absence? Never mind. Come on back in. Growth and strengthening is the inborn direction of the spirit, too. It, too, makes up for lost time quickly. It, too, feels better when it's moving.*

How are the ice picks? Q asks when I come home from the gym. *Fine,* I answer, and all but bound up the stairs. It's the truth: I feel great. Almost normal. But after I've been sitting at the computer for only a half hour, they're back with a vengeance.

In the night, I creep from our bed and into the India Room, where the mattress is somehow gentler on my knee. I turn on the radio and let it lull me to sleep. Once in a great while I take an arthritis remedy that costs $150 for a month's supply. And we don't need a national prescription drug program.

The doctor says to pack it in ice. Or soak it in hot water. *Both?* I don't get it. I take glucosamine, the same thing we give to our arthritic cat. It seems to have fixed her right up, but I'm afraid I can't say the same. Just about the only thing that helps is changing the position of the leg constantly. It is as if I were trying to keep from petrifying.

There are photographs of ancient bones in the newspaper this morning. People had hard lives back then. A scientist points soberly to roughened patches on the tops of the old femurs. They seem oddly familiar. That's why my knee makes that gravelly noise when I bend it, I guess, bone against bone, with no nice smooth cartilage in between, anymore, to smooth things over. How unattractive. How prehistoric.

There are things I can do at the gym to make all this more bearable. I can lift a fifty-pound weight with my leg, bending at the knee, moving it up and down only slightly, to work the muscles around my knee. It is said that they will become tough and strong, and that they will hold the knee in place, like a girdle. I can keep going to yoga, and stretch in between yoga classes, and maybe the splinted feeling around the knee will improve. Maybe not.

Interestingly, one of the surgeries intended to alleviate the pain actually *is* sticking an ice pick into your knee, only it's not really an ice pick. It's a hollow needle. You get to watch, they say. I think I'd pass. Fortunately, I've just read that this particular surgery appears to avail little in terms of actual improvement to peoples' knees, so I am crossing it off my list of things to decide whether or not to do to myself. That just leaves a face lift and Botox.

Botox! You've got to love a beauty aid made of botulism. Looking at pictures of myself recently, I could see the two vertical lines between my eyes have deepened considerably. They're extremely mobile and eloquent. They certainly make me look . . . well, experienced. They also make me look a little bit skeptical, like I don't quite believe whatever it is I have just heard. That can come in handy.

I will not divulge the name of the fine actress I recently saw in a movie she made a couple of years ago. She played a sly eighteenth-century schemer of the best sort, conniving with a wicked male friend in the ruin of a young virgin. The settings were splendid, various palatial French *chateaux*, and the costumes were wonderful. Humanity has never dressed so well as it dressed in those days. Looking skeptical was just what one would want to do if one were playing such a character.

Except she couldn't: she didn't have her two vertical lines! She had an unbroken, unmoving expanse of white forehead. Her eyebrows did not move.

She couldn't raise one knowingly. It was as if her face were put together from two different faces, one that would move and one that was made of plaster. She smiled and laughed and curled her lips for all she was worth, but her forehead stayed exquisitely still. As a result, there was something decidedly puppet-like about her.

Poor thing. She probably looked at the two lines in the mirror and felt sad. Probably looked at all the twenty-year-olds getting roles they're too young to play and worried about work. So she called up the Botox people and zapped her skeptical lines. They'll come back. Botox only lasts a few months. Some folks in the business are actually getting injections of it in *between* jobs, so that they will wrinkle more slowly, and then letting it wear off so they can move their faces when they're working. All right.

What we can do to change our bodies is amazing. And what we can't do to change the basics of human life is almost everything. You can pump and pedal and jump and lift and still become ill from something you thought was strictly a punishment for couch potatoes. You can have the best obstetrician and not smoke or drink, you can listen to nothing but Mozart all through your pregnancy, and still end up two weeks late and needing a C-section. It's still a good idea to do these things. But we're not in charge.

Do you want to go back to the doctor? Q asks this morning as I lie in bed complaining about my knee. *Nah,* I say. *There's really nothing more to do. I'll go rake some leaves and get the kinks out.*

Maybe someday I'll have a shiny new titanium knee with deluxe Teflon fake cartilage. I'll set off airport metal detectors and be escorted into curtained areas with other silver-haired women: the terrorist grandmothers. It's a piece of cake, people who have had their knees replaced say. Some of them. Others are a little quieter about the ease of replacing such a complicated joint. They don't replace your knee until you're a lot worse off than I am.

I'm looking forward to it. I wish I could see what my leg looks like at the moment it doesn't have a knee—that must look very odd. I wish I could know what it is like to have an almost instant relief from a pain that has been a constant companion. *Haven't had a bit of pain ever since I had it done,* person after person tells me, slapping a knee or patting a hip. Wow.

Can you have your neck replaced? I ask Q in the night. I can't get comfortable. We each have one of those pillows that are supposed to be kind to the neck. I find them agonizing. I think of having some of my neck removed, perhaps the whole thing, of letting my head just sit on my shoulders.

How terrible would that be, really? I wouldn't be able to look behind me, but is there really anything back there I want to see?

Q says he doesn't believe they're doing neck replacements.

I used to flop in a chair. Now I sit carefully. I used to run down the stairs. Now I creep. I used to be a dancer. I'm not now. I didn't even notice what kind of mattress or pillow I had in the old days. Now I seem obsessed with my bedding, always in the market for a magical pillow, longing for a featherbed. I've changed a lot since the old days.

And shouldn't a person be able to remember on Friday that she's directing a show on Sunday? A person should be able to remember in the morning what she did the night before. A person should be able to remember whether or not she's taken her pills.

I don't remember any of these things. I thought it would improve once I retired. *It's stress,* I told myself; *I'm working too hard.* But now I am all but motionless and it's getting worse and worse. I enter a room and am unable to say why I am there. I go out and come in again, hoping it will jog my memory. Sometimes it does. At other times—nothing.

My friends all worry secretly about Alzheimer's disease. They take ginkgo biloba and wonder if it's at all for real. Silently, they monitor their memory

lapses and wonder what they mean. They're afraid
to ask anybody but themselves. Is this the beginning of the end? Today I can't remember what I
made a special trip out to the store to buy. Tomorrow will it be my children's names?

Actually, I'm ahead of the game. I've been
forgetting my children's names for years. Grand-
children's too, now. I scroll through a mental
pull-down menu every time I want one of them,
stopping at the right one when it comes around:
Corinna . . . uh, Anna . . . no, Rose . . . Madeline
. . . I've done this for as long as there have been
more than one of them. Twenty-eight years.

And is there a way to write with dignity about
urinary incontinence?

I thought not. Am I alone, furtively rinsing out
my underwear and stockings in public restrooms,
glued to my seat, backing out of rooms to hide the
evidence of my lack of physical control?

I am not alone. Bring it up and fifty-some-
things are on it like locusts, laughing, one-upping
each other with their remembered humiliations,
which they trot out like the souvenirs of a vacation.
I have learned to spot fellow sufferers: determined-
looking people walking fast through public places,
grimly in search of the nearest convenience, hearts
sinking when they find one at the end of a long
line of anxious souls. Shrill laughter goes up from

a men's room in which there are no men: the girls have taken it over, and cackle loudly—too loudly. They are embarrassed.

My memory of this health problem is that old people had it. I remember my grandmother's lingering death from cancer, through a long, hot summer. I remember being sent to the general store to buy rolls of quilt batting to lay under her wasting body, remember my mother and cousin turning her, sliding a fresh length of the softness under her, taking the soiled one away, burning it in a barrel way out in the back yard, far away from the house. *Could we roast marshmallows in the fire?* I asked, interested and hopeful. *No,* my mother said, in such a tired voice, *not in this fire.*

I should remember before setting out somewhere that I have this problem. That's what the Queen of England always does, I have read: she instructs her family to use a restroom every time they see one, just in case. Excellent advice. The monarchy should be retained. I don't take the queen's advice, though. I always forget. I bought some pads—smaller versions of the roll of quilt batting. They are brand-named "Poise," a name which, I think, doth protest too much, suggesting that the pads will counter the animal reflex I can no longer control. Good idea. The Poises sit on the bathroom shelf. I forget all about them.

On the phone, I tell Anna about a mishap earlier in the day. "You should wear those pads you bought, Mom," she says matter-of-factly. Anna is right. I should. But I don't. I'm not used to planning on being less than I was. I have always planned on being more.

I was precocious in this regard: it began in my early forties, suddenly, when I was hit by a car. I sustained many small fractures in my spine and pelvis, which left me a little crooked and a little nerve damaged. "We just want the jury to understand that you're not who you were," said my lawyer when I found it tedious to let expert witness doctors examine me for the trial. So I let them: they measured nerve conduction in my damaged leg, ordered MRIs and bone scans, gauged my walking, measured my muscle atrophy. But I didn't tell any of the expert doctors about my sudden embarrassments. "Why didn't you tell me?" my lawyer asked in frustrated disbelief after the trial. "We would have won a helluva lot more money." I had no good answer to this reasonable question. It never occurred to me to bring it up.

I was not brought up to talk that way. My mother used to spell things; *Oh, D-A-M-N!* she would say. She was squeamish about words that referred to the human body: we had *bosoms,* not *breasts,* and neither of us ever had occasion to use the word *vagina*. I would be more relaxed, I promised myself. My first child chose the ono-matopoeic *tinkle* to describe urinating, a word she got not from me but from her nursery school teacher. Only she hadn't heard it quite right: twin-kle was what she said, leaving me to wonder what image presented itself in her imagination when we sang "Twinkle, Twinkle, Little Star." Her kids just say *pee*.

As does my husband, the most matter-of-fact person about biology with whom I have ever lived, unembarrassed by anything. Inconvenienced, per-haps, but not embarrassed. "What's that there for?" a grandchild asks, pointing to a broken-off zipper pull, detached, in a moment of true emer-gency, from a pair of trousers. Q has taped it to the front of the dashboard in our car. It has stayed there for several years. "It's a reminder that life is uncertain," he answers. "That's really weird," the grandchild says. Maybe. Maybe not. The grand-children have never found themselves standing with a shuttered fly and the zipper pull come away in their hands. Q and I share this humbling bond, as if we were contemporaries, when he is actually ever so much older than I am. "Guess what hap-pened to me today," I say tragically as I get into his waiting car at the train station. "What? he says."

"Three guesses."

"Oh, honey, that's too bad," he says, and I am immensely comforted. A strange bond to have with one's lover. But an endearing one.

Stiff. Sore. Wrinkled. Forgetful. Short on energy. Orthopedic of shoe, with a dozen pairs of high heels sighing to themselves in the closet. Occasionally, embarrassingly, incontinent. But oddly unconcerned about any of these things. I'm not what I was in many ways. But not in every way. I am still many things I was in the old days. And I am also a few things I wasn't then. A few good things.

Some things you just have to live with. Make them better any way you can, and then turn your attention to other things for as long as you can. I may have a bad knee, but that's not the same thing as *being* one. My neck may hurt, but I don't have to be a pain in one. I'm lots of things, even if, sometimes, I have a hard time remembering what some of them are. But no, don't help me. They'll come to me.

Turn That Thing Down!

Frank and I spent every Saturday night together for years. He sang; I was content just to listen. WNEW played Frank's records from eight to midnight for years, and my preferred way to spend Saturday night was in bed with the radio, listening to songs about not having a sweetheart. Or about having had one and gotten dumped. Or about being unable to play well with others: Frank always had to do it His Way.

On weeknights, it was WQXR. Nimet was—and still is—on late at night. Heralded by Debussy's *En Bateau,* she sails into the studio at midnight and stays there until five-thirty in the morning.

Nimet speaks with an indeterminate accent. She is Egyptian by birth but has lived in many parts of the world, and she has absorbed a bit of the accent of each one. She giggles girlishly from time to time, although she cannot have been a girl for decades; she's been on the radio for years and years. Giggles or no, she is a top-drawer musicologist with very catholic tastes. I would fall asleep to Stravinsky and awaken at three to Gilbert and Sullivan, without a clue as to how I had gotten from one to the other.

I was still single when I was hanging out with Frank and Nimet. The old gang kind of broke up, though, when I married Q. Q can't stand the radio on when he's trying to sleep. He keeps trying to *listen*: he can't let it lull him. So my radio days are over. Except on the nights when I can't sleep. Then I arise and sneak off to the guest room, where I hit the *on* button, and the BBC surfaces. I count on it when I wake up and can't go back to sleep. It works better than any pill. They start in with the daily chant of international cricket scores, and I drift off.

Listening to the BBC when nobody else is awake is like being a child at home, nestled in a pile of coats while the grownups talk in the next room. I don't really hear what they say. I don't try to. It's enough to know that they are there.

Or like lying in my bed upstairs and listening to my parents and older brothers still awake downstairs, drifting off to the clatter of washing dishes, footsteps on the stairs, the closing of doors, voices. I was a little afraid of the dark in those days, but the sounds of family life going on downstairs let me know I was not alone. It was enough to know that they were there.

It's like lying awake at night in New York and listening to the people come and go on the street below. The audio snatches of their lives as they pass by are a lullaby. After a time, you don't even notice when they're too loud. It's enough to know that they are there.

It's like listening to many sermons: a chance to let the mind wander where it will, while the preacher drones earnestly on and on. Preachers today must work to pierce the armor of exhaustion and attention deficit modern people wear to church, and not every cleric wields the sharpest of swords. You may suspect that yours is in need of whetting if people frequently shake your hand at the door and say "Thank you for your message," which really means *I don't remember a single thing you said, but you seem like a lovely person, and I know you did your best.* Don't worry, though, even if this occurs regularly. Be of good cheer. Your effort is not wasted. People today need their rest.

It is enough for them to know that you are there.

The BBC is one of the more benign legacies of empire, matter-of-fact in its assumption that its listeners are all over the world. It corrects the parochialism of American broadcasting, with its African and Indian and Nepalese and even Irish accents sprinkled among the English ones.

And it's not just the accents. I like to hear what things look like to people in other places. Our news people travel overseas, too, but they remain American wherever they go, and they're talking to Americans. Hearing the news is a different experience when that's not the case. It's not a bad idea for us to get a feel for what the world is like when it's not all about us. I am soothed, sometimes, by the sound of the world carrying on without me, to feel the size of the world, its variety of people, to feel other time zones.

Something funny is happening to me now, though. Lately, sometimes, the BBC doesn't work for me. I think I'm becoming like my husband, losing my ability to be lulled by sound. I used to be able to drift off, but now my mind is pricked by what I hear. I seem to be losing my liking for cuddling up on a pile of adult coats and half-listening to conversation that doesn't include me. It seems no longer to make me feel secure, not every time. Sometimes it makes me feel annoyed.

I used to be able to read or study with music on. I had different symphonies for different subjects: Beethoven's *Ninth* for history, Sibelius's *Finlandia* for literature. Stravinsky's *Symphony of Psalms* for theology. It used to help me concentrate. It covered other noise.

But sometimes, now, it distracts me. Sometimes, now, I can't listen and do something else. I have to just listen. Or turn it off.

My older daughter came of age to heavy metal. Her sister loved Madonna. I didn't mind. Why would I? I grew up with rock and roll. But now I can't drive and listen to my granddaughters' hip-hop at the same time. And sometimes, alone in the car, I don't want to hear the oldies station play stuff by the Four Tops or the Righteous Brothers, or even the Beatles. It makes me feel nervous and tired, now, to listen and drive.

Hospital patients usually have the television on without even knowing it. I used to be able to talk with a patient in some depth while Oprah plied her trade in the background. Now I have to ask if we can turn it off. When I am a patient myself, I'd rather have my lungs suctioned than the television hooked up. If my neighbor elects the TV—they almost always do—I long for a private room.

What is happening to me? Where is the little girl who fell asleep with the television on in her brothers' bedroom and had to be carried to her own? Where is the teenager who lay under her flowered bedspread each night and listened attentively to dangerous songs, listened hard to Mick Jagger get no satisfaction and drifted off to dangerous dreams, before she knew much of anything about what satisfaction was?

That girl must have moved.

Or maybe it's something else. Maybe a paradox is happening.

Maybe I'm finding music distracting because I'm having trouble hearing it.

My grandmother, a music teacher, was deaf in her old age. So was my father. My brother, not much older than I am, is very hard of hearing.

"What do you mean, you wish you were dead?" I ask Q, alarmed. He hasn't seemed depressed to me.

"I said 'I'm going to *bed*.'" he says.

"Oh."

This is happening to both of us. The results can be amusing.

"What do you mean, thirty feet? It's only about eighteen inches long," I say, holding a small trellis aloft in the garden.

"No, I said it has *dirty feet*," he says, pointing to the mud on the bottom of the trellis.

"Oh."

"You used to sit on a bubble?" he says, puzzled.

"No, no, I'm sorry to be such a *trouble*."

"Oh, *trouble!*"

I make an appointment with an ear doctor. I sit in a soundproof booth and raise my hand every time I hear a high-pitched sound. I know my right ear is better than my left: I've been changing from left to right on the telephone for years. But the doctor says my hearing is normal and sends me home. He tells me I should try to listen more carefully. What a good idea. Why didn't I think of that?

I *hear* sound. But *defining* sound is becoming difficult. That is why I have trouble with music in the background sometimes. It no longer pours into my ears in a strong, clear stream. It *creeps* in now, uneven, muffled, unclear. I must strain to understand it, spending energy I didn't used to need for this purpose.

When Beethoven was my age, he had been deaf for twenty years. Not all deafness is silent: sometimes the deaf experience tintinitis, persistent sounds in the ears, steady and continuous enough to threaten madness. Beethoven had it. The works he composed in this condition rank among the world's great works of genius. So undistracted was he that he could hold staff upon staff of notes in his head and hear them in his imagination, all with terrible, whining un-music in his ears. A hateful combination: too much of one unwelcome sound, none of the sound for which he longed.

He had to learn to be that undistracted. At first, stricken in his early thirties, his career as a concert pianist in defeat because of it, he prayed for death. Gradually, though, his stubborn genius reasserted itself. Most music lovers would rank his later works—all the symphonies but the first, all the string quartets—above the ones he completed while still a hearing man. His age and experience, his fierce determination, and his genius won out over his limitation.

You may have a disability. You *will* develop one, if you live long enough. But you needn't *become* your disability. I am not a genius like Beethoven. But I can summon what wit I have and navigate through the shoals of my weaknesses, because wit will trump weakness in the end.

By the time my father died, I really had to speak up if I wanted him to hear me. When I speak softly now, my brother cannot hear me. It is hard not to hear. *I was forced to isolate myself. I was misunderstood and rudely repulsed because I was as yet unable to say to people, "Speak louder, shout, for I am deaf,"* wrote Beethoven about the early days of his impairment. I may be like that, too, someday.

On a bus downtown, I sit behind a group of teenagers. They are shouting and laughing, like teenagers always do on a bus—but they are silent. I know they are shouting because of the rapidity of their hand movements, their big grins, the way they interrupt one another, poke each other, demanding the floor. Kids.

I was forced to isolate myself.

Speak louder. Shout, if you must, while I can still hear you. What did you say?

Somebody Call Me Mama

She tries not to show it, but I can tell that my daughter really doesn't want to do this. A slight unevenness in selling one house and buying another has left her and her gang in between homes for six weeks. They have come to stay with us. She appreciates the hospitality, but I understand her reluctance—who wants to go and live with her mom when she's all grown up? She looks into a few hotel rooms. But it will only be for a few weeks, and the thought of living with two teenagers in a hotel room is even worse than the thought of going home to Mom.

I will make it as easy for her as I can. I will work to ensure that she doesn't feel like a kid again. We have room. I can make things better for my daughter and her girls. My mother wasn't alive to do that for me, but I am alive. Thank God.

I am excited. Children in the house again! Well, not children—teenagers. I doubt if this is much fun for them, actually. The girls share the India Room, which is definitely on the small side, and their mom is on the living room couch. But it's wonderful for me. To have them at our table makes me happy. To have them tucked in at night, however cramped their sleeping arrangements, makes me feel safe. And these six weeks will include both Thanksgiving and Christmas: Thanksgiving cooking with a whole brood, Christmas morning, baking cookies, hiding gifts, everything. I can't wait.

You never get over having had them. You never forget the day-to-day morning-ness and evening-ness of them, the steady stream of life that a houseful of people brings into yours. I see now that Q and I have become very quiet, our days almost stately in their predictable unfolding. Even What's-Her-Name has developed a routine of life, albeit not one that could ever be called stately: her own bowl, her own opportunity to steal food from Kate after finishing her own breakfast, her own intent circuit of the house to find a window with a person in the room behind

it, outside of which she can suddenly appear and
beg entry. Now she is jarred out of her compla-
cency: they have brought their dog, and the dog
trots around the house, her claws clicking on the
wooden floors, eating the cats' food, noisily drinking their water, startling What's-Her-Name, forc-
ing a revision of her days.

And of mine. For no good reason, I am late
with the day's writing and prayer. Morning Prayer
is usually at five-thirty or six. Today it was at
nearly nine o'clock, after the last one had left for
school. It was hard to put it first with kids in the
house. It was like the old days—pulled from prayer
and writing by other things. Not pulled: attracted.
By attractive things: fixing breakfast, sending people out the door. Attractive things. Good things
that will not come again: they will not be young
again, these girls. They will probably never live
here again. This is probably my last chance.

What did they need? Nothing serious—wake-
up calls with only moderate begging, rides to school
from Q , lunch money, then *forgotten* lunch money
that has Q driving back to the school again to drop
it off in the principal's office. None of it is rocket
science. Just the daily stream of life with young
people in the house.

Q and I did not have children. We came to
each other already supplied. So I have no memory

of his taking our kids to school. He took his own, long ago, decades before we met. I wish we had met earlier. His participation in these daily rituals of parenthood is new to me, then, new and lovely, like so many others: sitting at the dinner table, thinking about what to buy at the store, about who is driving whom, and where.

Often they are not where we think they are.

We prepare a dinner and they are nowhere to be found.

I ask one to get up and get ready for school and return ten minutes later to the same motionless lump. Why do adolescents have to be at school so early? They should start their school day at noon and stay there until six.

We tell them to do something and they forget. They eat cookies and then don't want their dinner. They watch too much television. They need something and forget to tell us, necessitating a special trip to the store, back to the school in mid-morning. They are thoughtless, Q says. I think back. Well, yes, I suppose they are. Mine were teenagers more recently than his were. Maybe his weren't thoughtless. These two are like mine. What goes around appears to be coming around, just like they always say it does.

They are thoughtless, says Q. But he gets into the car and goes, anyway.

We have summit meetings around the dinner table about the issues that come up when a number of people live together in the same not-so-enormous house. The idea is that we will first express appreciation for something they have done well and then talk about things that need to happen differently. We do this better sometimes than we do at other times. Sometimes it seems our litany of things that should be different—glasses that need to be put in the dishwasher, clothing that needs to be hung up, shopping lists that need to be updated, this, that—is much too long. We drone on and on with it, and I can see their eyes glaze over. Right now, for instance, I can't remember what the appreciation we expressed this evening was about, exactly. I think we may have left it out.

Their presence is oddly tiring. The television is in my office, and I find it harder to write when they are watching it than I used to when I was younger. This makes me sad: it seems that I should be able always to rejoice in the presence of children I love so much. But this is unrealistic: they do not always rejoice in me. Nobody always rejoices in anybody, except God, I suppose, and even God must become annoyed with us sometimes.

When mine were little, I used to escape them by rising early to study and write. It was self-defense: when they were awake, I was fair game. I developed a permanent early rising habit, one that has served me well ever since. Probably I will revert to it tomorrow, so I can be theirs when they need me. Probably the silence of the early morning will again draw me from our warm bed into my tiny office. Probably I will realize, as I realized long ago, that I can do both: be a mom and be a person of prayer and study.

Or perhaps they won't need me. Because I am a mom, but I'm not their mom. They have a mom. I'm their grandmother. I am not the central figure in their lives. I'm the one on the edges. A grandmother swoops in now and then and makes things better, if she can. A grandmother is an extra pair of hands for a mother or a father. A grandmother is another head. A grandmother brings history with her.

She must never do any of these things explicitly, though. She must give her gifts invisibly, for the young need to feel that their wings are unfolding naturally, that they are traveling on their own road at their own pace, not being dragged along someone else's road. Nobody wants her advice, not if it's presented as advice. Nobody wants the lessons of her history if they are presented as lessons. People don't even always want her recipes, not if they're presented as the only right ones. People want to try things for themselves, the way the grandmother did when she was young. So the grandmother must sit on her hands, often, while things that one might have predicted would turn out poorly—turn out poorly.

And sometimes she notices that they don't turn out poorly at all, that they turn out rather well. Better than it looked like they would when she was still trying to micromanage them.

And sometimes she is flattered by a sudden flush of accomplishment: they like her piecrust, they like her silver, they think something she says is funny. They go through the house and put round stickers on all the things they want to inherit when she dies. This is great fun. She remembers rock and roll songs from when they came out the first time. They are impressed at this. She remembers music their mother liked when she was a teenager. They like this music, too, in a way. Oldies, they call it.

She remembers wishing for a boyfriend and not having one. She remembers firmly believing she never would have one, and also believing that she would be the only girl in history who never grew breasts, who never menstruated. She would be a freak. She remembers that youth is not always a delight for the young. She remembers the pain of not measuring up to standards that she knew, even at the time, to be superficial. She remembers doing stupid things for no good reason. She remembers acting against what she knew was best for her, doing things she knew were wrong, out of her longing to fit in with other people. She remembers thinking she could do things she could not do, thinking things would not hurt her the way they hurt other people. She remembers being angry when these things were pointed out to her. *They think I'm stupid,* she muttered to herself.

I'm not stupid, my granddaughter says scornfully when I'm trying to warn her about something dire. No. You're so bright you scare me. But you are so young.

Paradise Regained

The What's-Her-Name Chronicles

Ⅰt's very early. Usually I'm up and writing by five A.M., a habit I developed when my children were small and just couldn't let me work when they were up. The rule in middle age is that anytime after four A.M. I can get up. If it's earlier than that, I stay in bed. So, sometime after four, I arise, turn on the computer, say Morning Prayer while the machine is struggling to awaken, and then write the day's meditation.

A bump and a scuffling at my office window make me jump. *What the—?* It's still dark. My window is twenty feet off the ground. I'm not expecting anyone.

It's What's-Her-Name. She has seen the feeble glow of the computer screen from the ground, climbed the tree outside the window, leapt across six feet of thin air over a twenty-foot drop, and landed precariously on the edge of the roof, still three feet below the window. I open the screen. She looks reproachfully up at me, as if I were the cause of her trouble, then gathers herself and leaps, easily gaining the window ledge. With a *plunk* she hits the office floor and stalks off into the bedroom without so much as a thank-you.

I hope this doesn't become a trend, I think grimly as I struggle to close the screen. Now both cats know I'm up. They cry for food in the kitchen now, frantically shoving their heads into their bowls while I try to fill them, so that I can barely get the food in, then setting upon it as if they hadn't eaten for a week. An hour or so later, when I am safely upstairs at the computer and Q comes downstairs, they tell him that they haven't eaten yet and are really hungry. After their second breakfast, they are ready to begin the day.

Kate goes out to the back yard to secure the perimeter. She takes a brief tour and then finds a nice secluded spot for a nap, one in which she can't be seen—her tortoiseshell coat blends in beautifully with the base of a hedge, the base of the rose bushes by the house—but from which she can see everything. She alternates between sleep and watching the garden.

What's-Her-Name is younger and more adventurous: she goes hunting. It has been a dangerous summer for mice and birds on the Geranium Farm: a couple of weeks ago, we were finding former mice just about every day. Last week I went out front and the birdbath was on its side. As I righted it, I saw five or six tailfeathers clinging to the rim. *What's-Her-Name was here.* The corpse was nowhere to be found. She must have lurked in the echinacea and then pounced on an unwary bather.

Another former mouse in the driveway this morning. There was one there yesterday, too. What's-Her-Name is at the back door, complaining again about not having had breakfast yet. This would be her third.

Why don't you eat your mouse? Q asks her. She tosses a scornful meow over one shoulder and stalks in when he opens the door. *Dance,* I say playfully, holding the bowl above her head. She always dances for Q when he feeds her. She looks at me as if I've lost my mind. I put the bowl down and make a hasty retreat.

I don't know why she doesn't eat the mouse she caught this morning, or the one she left there yesterday, or the bird she got yesterday afternoon. I guess *eating* the mouse is not the point of her mouse hunts. It's just the thrill of the chase. Anyway, What's-Her-Name sure is on a roll these days; not bad for a cat with no front claws. Whoever had her before we got her had her declawed and then abandoned her. That's a terrible thing to do, leaving a cat outside without her natural defenses. It doesn't seem to have slowed What's-Her-Name down any, though. I've seen her run up a tree trunk, all the way to the top in two seconds, all without any claws in front with which to cling.

What should we do about the birds and the mice? Should we stop her? I came face to face with her the other day with a live baby squirrel in her mouth. A baby! That seemed too much to bear. Q and I gave chase, egged on by the squawks of the mother squirrel. But you can't catch a cat who doesn't want to be caught. Into the underbrush she vanished, the struggling squirrel still in her mouth. We went inside so we wouldn't have to hear the rustle of the branches as she played with it.

It's their nature, to hunt. It's a reminder, to those of us who tend to romanticize nature, that violence is integral to it. *Why can't we be like the animals and all get along?* we think as we scan the scary headlines. Hah! We *are* like the animals. They catch and kill a mouse or a bird they don't want to eat. We involve ourselves in escalating projects of violence, paint ourselves into corners we hate, and in the end, can't really say why we do so other than that it's to preserve our freedom. But sometimes I wonder if that's really true. Why do we fight so much in the name of peace? Why do we seem to prefer it? Is there something in us *like* what is in them, something that enjoys the thrill of the chase more than we might ever be comfortable admitting, to ourselves or to anybody else? I hope not, but I fear so.

Of course, we are not only like them. We are also, we believe, like God in some way. *Made in the image of God,* we say. We may love the thrill of the chase, but we also have within ourselves the capacity to transcend it, to choose beyond and above it. We may build a bomb, but we also write a poem. Some people do both. But all of us can choose the manner in which we deploy who we are in the world. We can decide how we will be true to our natures.

Over the years, we have compiled a great store of mythology about the cats. We attribute our own emotions and motivations to them, as if they were human. I am convinced that Kate resents me for marrying Q. Because it's such a good story, I have found all manner of data to support that belief. We think What's-Her-Name is something of a juvenile delinquent, and so it seems to us that she acts like one. Their turf wars seem theological to us, as they probably do not to them: deep-seated controversies about personal worth and tradition.

We deliberately misunderstand them. Because it's funny.

Sometimes we misunderstand people, too, in ways that are maybe not so funny. We think we know what someone else wants and needs. We think we know what they think: *They think what we think.* We think we know where they've been. Because we have known someone in the past, we think we know his present, her future, his thoughts, her beliefs. We create people according to knowledge we think we have. People and animals: we create them in our own image.

We even do that to God. We think God hates what we hate, shares our prejudices. We think that God cannot understand or encompass what is beyond us. *And you think that I am like you,* God says in a psalm.

God is nothing like us. We really haven't a clue.

Anthropomorphizing the cats is fun. More fun, though, is just watching them and liking them, touching them when they will permit it, taking our cues from their odd ways. Assuming we know all about our fellows makes us feel secure, but letting them reveal themselves on their own terms is both more respectful and productive of a more accurate

vision of them. To praise God as if God were a
larger version of ourselves keeps us in the comfortable realm of the familiar. But the holy and the
familiar are not the same.

A loud crash and the tinkle of breaking glass
the next night.

Neither of us springs out of bed, though. We
don't even grunt. One word crosses my mind as
sleep settles over me again after this momentary
interruption: *What's-Her-Name.*

Maybe that's three words.

And in the morning, when I yield to the cats'
entreaties and go downstairs to fix their breakfast,
I see that she has knocked the lovely apple pie I
had made the other day onto the floor, breaking
the glass pie plate in which it sat on the counter.
Fortunately, it was enclosed in a plastic bag, so
glass didn't go all over the kitchen. Now we have a
bag of glass and pie.

You jerk.

She is why we put the pie in a plastic bag to
begin with. The last pie I made, a nice rhubarb, sat
out naked and she ate the top crust off one night.

Jerk. Cats don't eat pie.

This one does.

She and Kate attack their bowls. The cat food
looks particularly vile this morning, Chicken and
Salmon Dinner in Gravy, for heaven's sake, and

soon Kate has had her fill. What's-Her-Name polishes off her own and goes over to finish up Kate's. Kate asks to go outside for a walk, but What's-Her-Name stays inside, staring fixedly at the basement door. She creeps up to it and waits. *There's nothing for you down there*, I say to her sternly, not yet willing to let the pie be bygones.

But then I remember that maybe there *is* something for What's-Her-Name down in the basement, that I saw a tiny gray furry body in the garden alongside the house yesterday, and that it disappeared as I watched—into the foundation. The weather is turning. The mice are coming inside.

Oh, What's-Your-Name, I sing seductively. *He-ere, kitty, kitty.*

I open the door and she bounds down the stairs, disappearing into the darkness. Soon she tears back up and dashes around the corner into the living room, with something in her mouth. I hear her thunder up the stairs, pause, and then thunder back down. She gallops through the house, turning back the corners of rugs, running into walls, the racket she makes punctuated by periods of pregnant silence: she has released her prey and is allowing it to try to get away. Then a scuffle: she pounces, and gallops off again. I prop the back door open invitingly. *Take that thing outside.*

If the mice know there's a good hunter in the house, they may take up residence elsewhere while the weather is still warm enough to make the move. This would be good. It would go a ways toward redeeming the pie.

They said on the radio this morning that growing up in homes with cats and dogs may make children less susceptible to all common allergens. They studied children in a middle-class suburb near Detroit, thinking that having animals in the house was related to childhood allergies, and found that the statistical opposite was true.

I'm glad to hear this. It's about time the cats did some work around here. If they've been helping children with their allergies all this time, though, I've misjudged them and I'm sorry. It's just that you can't really tell when a cat is working. It looks like they're sleeping. I've often mistaken a cat putting in a long day of painstaking allergy prevention for one taking an eighteen-hour nap.

The radio show was illuminating, and personally affirming. It turns out dirt is good for you. Keep things too clean and you become delicate, and every little thing sets you off.

Hepatitis? Tetanus? Pneumonia? Malaria? Diphtheria? the nurse was checking off my immunizations. Yes, yes, yes, yes, and yes. We both got shot up to our gills when we went to India, and all our inoculations are still productively aswim in our bloodstreams. In India, Americans anointed themselves with antibacterial goo from little squeeze bottles, which they carried with them like rosaries everywhere they went. They talked over cocktails about their strategies for avoiding disease: *Don't touch anything, don't touch anyone, don't shake hands. And don't look the beggars in the eye. They'll grab hold of you and touch you.*

But I couldn't bring myself to sweep like a queen through a gauntlet of poor people. And I didn't have enough money for all of them. But I *could* touch them, and I did: just a hand on a shoulder, a smile and a nod, an expression of regret that I couldn't be of financial help at that moment. And yes, they touched me back. And some of them were very insistent, and I had to peel a clutch of fingers off my shoulder sometimes. But, although some of them were very dirty, I didn't get sick and die.

You become able to withstand sickness and trouble by becoming familiar with it. You're vulnerable to it if you show your fear. We're too estranged from the actual physical world, Americans, as if we were strangers in it and didn't really live here. Scared of dirt, scared of the sun, scared of water, scared of germs. Scared of doing something new. Scared of getting sick. Scared of life. So we live lives of avoidance, and in the end, we die anyway.

I say the hell with it. When your number's up, your number's up, and a lion's going to eat you up while you're walking down the street, no matter what. Do what you can to be all right, but don't make staying alive your life's work. Your life's work should be something else, something larger than you, something that will be here when you are here no longer. And something wider than you, too, something that touches other people. If my tombstone were to sum me up in this way: *She was very, very careful all her life and then she died*—I'm not sure I'd view my life as much of a success.

Only you can touch others as you touch them. No one else will ever be able to do that but you. Don't deprive the world of your touch out of fear for your life.

After all, fear isn't necessarily a permanent state of mind. A case in point:

It might have been the *Fegato alla Veneziana*. I have no business eating calves' liver. Or a glass of wine *and* an Italian *aperitivo*. No need for that, either. Freud would have said it was the play we saw beforehand, a play as good as "A Streetcar Named Desire," one of the best I've ever seen, a production in which both characters are completely naked onstage a fair amount of the time and you see . . . everything. For whatever reason, I dreamed last night of a forty-foot snake.

What is profoundly odd is that it was a good dream. The snake was an anaconda, native to South America, shiny and black and very, very large. It had been pulled out of its lair by South American villagers, who wanted it to stop ravaging their village—this I had seen on "Animal Planet" once—and somehow it was temporarily in our house. *Oh, dear,* I thought when I saw it. I don't like snakes.

What's-Her-Name came in, though, and began to tear madly around the house, the way she does in pursuit of a mouse or a bug. The snake gave chase, but What's-Her-Name zigged and zagged, feinted and attacked, leapt, stood still, and pounced until the snake was exhausted and utterly dispirited. It was no match for What's-Her-Name. Nobody ever is.

It slid over to me and put its head in my bosom, plainly wanting comfort. I patted it. I looked at its forty-foot body curling all around the living room. I sighed and knew it was going to become a member of the family. I wondered how Q would take the news. A forty-foot snake was not something I could just bring in the house and hope he wouldn't notice.

The play was about a man and a woman and their exploration of whether or not they could love each other. As it opens, he's sure they can and she knows they can't. She has scars from her life that make her afraid of love. So, it turns out, does he. But it doesn't stop him from hoping and striving for it. Slowly, she also gathers the courage to hope, too. Lovely. Lovely.

I disliked snakes. And yet a forty-foot one invaded my living room in a dream and hoped for succor from me, and I found it within myself to give it.

Sometimes we change and heal. Sometimes we move through our fear into love. Sometimes we can do things we don't think we can do. Sometimes we love things that are really annoying.

What's-Her-Name would not be nearly so interesting an animal if she weren't such a pain. Her infuriating choices provide such a window into her aspirations as to make her seem almost rational. Almost emotional, in a human sense. She reminds me of myself. I locate my own sins and foolishnesses readily in her. They are less heart-breaking there.

Want a kitten? I ask Tom on the train. He doesn't say no outright. It is not What's-Her-Name for whom we seek new lodgings, although that's a tempting thought. It is the three remaining gray tabbies of Gypsy's litter, who are now about eight weeks old and very cute. It is too soon to predict their characters in any detail. We make no guarantees: after all, What's-Her-Name was innocent once.

It's too soon to predict almost anything. Almost anything into which we enter might be a disaster, or it might be the best thing that ever happened to us. Probably it will be neither of those. Probably, and most interestingly, it will just take its place in the parade of mixed experiences that composes a life.

I have never in my life not had a cat. I have never known what it is not to have an other around, a being whose ways confront me and assert her otherness, whose desires occasionally include me, whose animal warmth and odd initiatives enliven the house and inform the narrative of its occupants.

Surely it was for this delight that God created everything that is. To have an other. To have an initiative resembling the divine one, but not just the same. To have an unknown heart, a heart prepared to learn the way of revealing itself, a heart to which to reveal.

Within the three Persons of the mysterious Trinity, a conversation: *Did you hear that crash?*

What are they doing? . . . Who knows what they ever do? . . . They're so funny. . . . Look at that one. She's really pretty. . . . Look at him. I think he's hurt. . . . Look at those two. . . . Yeah, look. . . . I love having them with us. . . . Yeah, me too. . . . Yeah.

The Hummingbird
of Happiness

World Book Encyclopedia came to our house one afternoon in a truck. It was in several cardboard boxes, and it came with its own little wooden bookshelf where it would live. It was bound in blue cloth. Blue was my favorite color. Some volumes, like S, were fat. Other letters were so arcane that they didn't even have their own volumes, but had to share with other letters. This was the fate of Q, who had to share with P, and with W, X, Y, and Z, who all lived in the same apartment house at the end of the alphabet.

I hadn't known families could have encyclopedias. I thought only libraries could have them. I hadn't known we were going to get *World Book*. It just came one day after school. I was thunder-struck. The experience has stayed with me: to this day, I look forward with excitement to the arrival of the mail, even if I'm not expecting anything. Because it's just when you're not expecting anything that things happen.

Seldom, before or since, have I enjoyed anything as much as I did *World Book*. Its articles were brief and easy to read. I have looked at that edition as an adult, and see now that it was something less than scholarly in tone and was, on occasion, rather distressingly biased in favor of American-style capitalism. But a five-year-old thought it was perfect. Most of all, I loved the pictures. *World Book* didn't skimp on them; it knew what kids loved. In the D volume I came across a fulsome article under "Dress," with three wonderful pages of national costumes throughout the ages and around the globe. I never tired of looking at them, never wearied of imagining myself in some other time and some other place, looking very different from the way I looked in real life. I would be Spanish, with a mantilla and a comb, or a Renaissance maiden, with an Elizabethan square hoop skirt and a stomacher and a lacy ruff. The straight up-and-down styles of the American teens and twenties seemed plain and sad to me in the nineteen-fifties, and the blue-suited paragon representing the forties looked a little too much like my mother, but Dior's New Look was glorious with its full skirts and wasp waists, and I was sold. To this day, one of my favorite things is to discover that somebody in a show somewhere needs a costume, at a moment when I have time to make one.

I didn't spend all my time with D. Sometimes, I would get S down off the shelf and look up snakes. I did this primarily to scare myself, and I now forget just why I wanted to do that. There were pictures of various kinds of snakes, including North American snakes, uncomfortably close to home, these: the copperheads, garter snakes, and blacksnakes we had in our part of the country. There were pictures of their fangs and their lidless, malevolent eyes. There was a picture of a man milking a rattlesnake of its venom. I would stare at it and imagine touching the deadly viper. I would put the book back in the shelf with relief. I could close the cover on the snakes anytime I wanted to. They would never slide silently from their home in the pages of *World Book* to invade my room. I was safe.

But my very favorite hours with *World Book* were spent with B. For "birds." There were drawings—of nests, of the different kinds of beaks and talons, of the skeletal systems of modern birds as compared with their dinosaur-like forebears. And there were several pages of beautiful color photographs of birds: birds in their nests, birds on the wing, birds on the water and in the grass, birds perched on tree limbs, heads back, singing. And birds dancing: birds dance when they want to get married.

Some of the birds in the pictures were also in our back yard. The fat robin, whose lovely pale blue egg once fell out of her nest and landed in the grass. The bluejay, who squawked and dived in the yard, hoping to frighten off other birds so there would be more food for him. The immense black crows, everywhere out in the country, four or five times the size of other birds. The buzzards who circled animals run over in the road, signaling the appetizing presence of roadkill to other buzzards. Little chickadees, and mourning doves, whose low trilling coo repeated itself over and over again for hours. The picture of the bluebird was my favorite—such a lovely blue, so delicate in her round nest nestled amid green leaves. In the photograph, she sat coyly on her eggs, one of which peeked out slightly from under her feathers. I looked for her in the yard. She was not there. *You don't see them here much,* my grandmother said. *Down south, more. Kentucky.* But birds migrate, I thought. Maybe a bluebird would come along on her way to somewhere else. Meanwhile, there were many others to occupy my mind.

Every spring at least one baby bird would find itself on the ground, mysteriously orphaned and not yet able to fly. These were starlings, my grandmother told me with a sniff, and she wouldn't let me to bring them in the house. She would give me a shoe box and I would fill it with tissue paper and a jar lid with water in it and whatever I thought the baby bird might like to eat. I remember providing a strand of spaghetti once. I would install the little bird in its new home, where it would sit in stolid and silent misery, its feathers ruffled and unkempt, and wait to die. This it usually did in a day or too. It always happened, and I was always surprised. Surprised and sad, although their passing gave us the opportunity for a bird funeral and a bird burial. *People of the mid-twentieth century in America used birds in their religious rites,* future archeologists who dig around our house will conclude. *They buried them in the yards around their houses as a symbol of the afterlife.*

I saw a tiny hummingbird only once, so small I thought it was a bumblebee and didn't believe my grandmother when she told me it was a bird. I looked it up in *World Book.* Sure enough.

To see and hear and love the birds requires no equipment and no money, but you do need one thing: time. You need time to linger and look, time to be still and let the song of the bird creep into your awareness, time to see a bird who doesn't particularly wish to be seen, time to lie in bed in first light and listen to them awaken. That is why my childhood love of the birds remained behind when I left home, along with the aging *World Book* in the wooden shelf I now recognized as cheap-looking. There were now many new things not in *World Book*: no Alan Shepherd, no John Glenn, no Jack Kennedy, no Robert Kennedy or Dr. King. No Vietnam, to speak of. The birds I left behind were unaware of how different the world was becoming; their world was much the same. After a while, though, even they noticed the change: great phalanxes of identical new homes where the woods had been, where the meadow behind our house had been, where the farm across the road had been. Fewer trees. Fewer weeds, with their insects and seeds. More people. Chemical rain. Funny air.

I was in rapid motion myself, in a city far from my home. Sometimes I would see their relatives: flocks of daring pigeons careering around the corners of buildings as if in response to a common signal, gulls along the Hudson River, egrets in the marshy Meadowlands outside the Lincoln Tunnel. I traveled to many places. In Amsterdam I saw storks. In India, I saw a bluebird at last, but it was a kind we don't have in North America, and a kingfisher, and an eagle. There, I heard the songs of birds in a way I had forgotten how to hear them: loud and multiple, crowds of birds calling to one another and singing to one another and imitating one another. I remembered, in India, how much I had once loved the birds here.

But in India, I was on vacation. In America, I was busy. No lying in bed listening for song. No pausing to look up at trees. A few years ago, we put a feeder up in the back garden just outside the kitchen window. Once in a great while I drank my tea there and saw a bird. Sometimes it was a cardinal. A pair of fat doves came often. But often I would not even finish my tea; *Look at the **time**!* I would say, and head for the train.

*Look at the **time**! Look at the **time**!* If a bird were watching me with an eye to studying me, he would view that phrase as my call. *I just saw a female North American Episcopal Priest,* he would say to his friend. *Look, there she is, over there in the house. Listen? Do you hear? They say "Look at the **time**! Look at the **time**!"* See? Hear that?

Actually, they would not *be* people watchers. They have no interest in us as subjects. They are too busy with their own absorbing lives, with getting enough food and raising their families. They only care if they think we might bother their nests. They are like I was: busy; driven. They have no choice but to be so.

I have a choice. Perhaps it is the breadth of our choices, more than anything, that separates us from the animals. So much the authors of our own destinies, we are fascinated with creatures who are not, whose behavior can be predicted because of what we know about where they live and what they need. They travel on schedule, eat predictable food, behave the same way as their fellows when they mate. They have little to decide. They are pure act.

So what, then, is the meaning of the large sheet of old plastic bag my husband saw protruding from the opening of one of the birdhouses? Half in the house and half out, it was obviously being dragged inside by the occupants. What for? Each species has its own nest design. You can tell whose nest it is by its shape and the materials used to make it. God didn't program any of them to build plastic nests, not that I know of. I have heard of birds who use the trick of dangling a snakeskin from their nesting places, so potential predators will think a snake has already invaded, and I have heard that they will sometimes use a piece of plastic wrap if that's what they find instead. Are these guys making a snake decoy? Are they threatening Q, who walks past their house with a frequency that concerns the parents and makes them fly to neighboring branches to scold him noisily. Or are they just a whole lot smarter than we think?

I think about the birds a lot again now that I am at home most of the time. I think and read about them as much as I used to when I was five. I read about what they like to eat and how to lure them into your garden. We go to the bird shop and buy special seed for them, special feeders, a bird bath. I plant things I think they will like.

Hummingbirds like trumpet-shaped flowers, flowers they can stick their long beaks into to sip out the nectar. They seldom perch to eat, as many birds do: they usually hover. They like the color red, and they can be fooled even by red ribbon tied to a plant. Down they will come, it says in the book. Of course, you have to have something for them to eat when they do come. I buy a tacky red plastic pie plate-looking thing and fill it with boiled sugar water. I change it religiously ever two days, so it won't ferment and make the humming-birds sick. I buy a second feeder for the front yard, an elegant Calder-looking mobile with three ruby glass globes, into which I put more sugar water. I make about a gallon of sugar water a week. I color the sugar water red, now, on the advice of a suc-cessful hummingbird hostess.

With regret, I report that I am not a successful hummingbird hostess. Not yet. Not a bird. Friends email me reports of their hummingbird visitors— digital photographs, even—and, for a moment, I

know the sin of covetousness. But I remain faithful
to the hope of hummers, faithful in the provision
of their nectar, happy, even, in the thought of
them, although I do not yet see them.

It is possible that I will never see them. It may
be that I will fill the dumb-looking pie plate feeder
and the elegant glass globes every two days for
years, may plant many sweet lilies in many tempting places, may tie clouds of red ribbons on innu-
merable branches, and never get a hummer.

It is odd that this thought is not a distressing
one. Perhaps it is enough that there *are* hummingbirds. Perhaps I can live with not having them
myself, although I would dearly love to welcome
them into our garden. It may be that the *hope* of the
hummingbirds is enough, that the chief delight is
in the anticipation of them. I would not be the
first person to persevere in hope and never see the
Promised Land. Perhaps it is the *promise,* and not
its fulfillment, in which we really delight.

The hummingbirds are on the wing south by
now, for sure. It said so in the *New York Times*;
they got their own Op-Ed piece, all about how
wonderful it is to have them in your yard. *The New
York Times. Et tu.*

I've been *trying* to entertain them all summer,
of course. Festooning our garden with irresistible
red balloons, boiling and cooling gallons of sugar

water and hanging it in tacky plastic feeders. But the hummers who have passed us by have clearly been intent on other things. They have been like Odysseus tied to the mast, like his sailors with their ears stopped against the siren song, when they passed over our yard. There has been no time to stop for me. They have a journey that does not include me.

As personal as it feels today, I know that it is not. It's not me. Their journey has never been about us. Forces older and more powerful than human planning impel them. They take to the air with urgency, signaled by a change in the light or in the air, perhaps not signaled at all, but responding instead to something within their tiny bodies, something that just knows what time it is.

They left Ithaca and Rome and Troy, Illium and Syracuse, leaving behind all the wistful classical names of towns in a land nothing like the Mediterranean lands that first knew those names. They don't care. There are no hummingbirds in the Mediterranean.

They stopped at Kykuit, not because it was a Rockefeller estate but because there were some trumpet vines there, full of nectar, and they needed to eat quickly so they could keep going. They don't know about money, and they don't know the Rockefellers.

They stopped at Sleepy Hollow, knowing nothing about Ichabod Crane but seeing some bright pink fuschia hanging on a porch.

They scanned Battery Park and found some flowers. They knew nothing about what happened there more than two hundred years ago, when battle ships appeared in the harbor and blood flowed on the Bowling Green.

They did not know about the World Trade Center. *How can they not know?* we think. *How can anybody not have heard?* It seems to us as if the moon knows. But the hummingbirds saw nothing in the hole that might be a flower, and so they did not descend. Maybe in a few years. They went to the Brooklyn Botanical Garden instead.

Down past Trenton, knowing nothing about Washington's troops there during the Revolution. Along the Delaware River were some flowers, so they stopped briefly and sucked sweet nectar from their throats.

That a charter of freedom had been written in Philadelphia two centuries ago interested them not at all, but there were flowers near the Art Institute, and they ate again and flew away. There were flowers at Valley Forge, too, so some of them stopped there.

Antietam, Appomattox, Richmond, Vicksburg— bloody ground. Blood is red, and they like red, but it is not the red of blood that the birds are after. It is the red of flowers, the sweetness they advertise. Our most terrible moments pass them right by. They are focussed on other things. At Fort Sumter they visit the gardens outside; they don't know about the human heartbreak of the war that began there, about how long the pain lasted and how universal it was, about how the nation is riven by it even now, all these years later. They don't know about nations. Only flowers, and the sun, and the dark and the light. And the need for food. And the need to keep going.

Their tiny bodies shoot onward through the sky, flying low, wings beating furiously, so fast the human eye cannot see their beating. Their tiny hearts pound too rapidly for us to distinguish between the beats. Their eyes scan the ground continuously, looking for something that might be a flower. They stop and feed. Then they must be on their way.

In the South the search for food is easier. They are closer to their destination. The lilies still bloom and invite them, the honeysuckles are still fresh and full. Plenty to eat, but no time to stay. They stop in Birmingham, in Selma, in Oxford, in Memphis, and they know nothing of what those names have meant to us. We do not concern them.

The Alamo: they don't remember. But there are many blooms there, and they stop to feed. In Mexico they are unaware of the gap between the rich and the poor, of the love-hate relationship of the people with their wealthy neighbor to the north. They have forgotten all about the neighbor to the north. And they've never known about wealth.

The pattern of life and its sustenance unfolds with or without us. Our sorrows, so final and resounding in our hearts, attract hardly any notice among other living things. It will be possible, when the time comes, for all of them to get along without us entirely.

I may not continue. We may not even continue. But the earth will continue. God made it out of nothing and made us out of it. Everything created has a beginning and an end. Whatever happens, it's going to be all right.

In the Garden

I had almost forgotten about the hundred narcissus bulbs I ordered a few months ago when the large carton appeared on the porch one day last week. It's a mix of several different kinds and colors of daffodils, certainly enough to provide a wonderful display in the spring. The company always ships things when it's time to plant them, and warns against delaying planting longer than two weeks. Okay.

But I steadfastly refused to begin planting the bulbs until I had finished the book I was working on, which was almost three weeks overdue. Finally, on a Friday, it is done. I will reward myself with an orgy of bulb planting on Saturday. I will do this instead of yoga class.

You can tuck bulbs four to six inches deep right next to other plants, plants that will come up later than daffodils do. Then, when the daffodils are finished and their leaves start looking the worse for wear, the other plants come up and hide their raggedness for the rest of the summer.

You don't want to plant daffodils in rows. You want to place them around the landscape in a fashion that you hope will look random, like God put them there. Some people actually toss out a handful at a time and bury them where they fall. I don't do this: I'm afraid I'll forget one, and I am not about to give a squirrel a free lunch.

You don't realize how hard it is for human beings to achieve randomness until you try to simulate it. We are inveterate planners and arrangers. It's hard for us to let things fall where they may. Harder still to let them lie there. But gardens have a depressingly careful look if you don't let them make some of their own decisions: too straight, too orderly, nature *curated*, as if it were not nature.

I stoop and rise, stretch and dig and water. I work up more of a sweat in the garden than I do rowing five thousand meters in the gym. Back and forth, to get bone meal and compost and bulbs, back and forth to get them again, over and over. Each hole gets a teaspoon or so of bone meal and a handful of beautiful compost, black with worm turds and scraps of rotted leaves. Compost is how God continues to renew the face of the earth. We might think it should be by means of something a little more poetic, but it's basically compost, the rotted remains of living things entering the digestive tracts of hardworking earthworms beneath the ground and emerging in form agreeable to the fussiest of plants.

Worm turds. They've made us what we are.

Compost is very poetic, Q says indignantly, when he reads that I said it wasn't. *Worm turds are beautiful. Look at that.* He sifts a handful of rich black through his fingers and smiles. It falls to the ground around the base of a plant and the worms go to work.

Everything is a candidate for compost. You need kitchen scraps: the things you leave on your plate, the peelings of vegetables, old banana skins. But you also need dead leaves, grass clippings, lighter materials to give the denser ones airy space around them in which to decompose. And in the end, it's all one.

You can even use paper. What is paper, after all, but recycled plants? Wood or rag, it all comes back to plants, ground up and wetted and spread out in sheets to dry, then cut into squares. The medium of our thoughts and our communication of them, chopped up fine and composted like everything else.

Each person at St. Luke's had a piece of paper and a writing implement. They sat in the parish hall and heard a reading about the attack on the World Trade Center and its aftermath the year before. Then, using their nondominant hand, the hand they normally do *not* use to write or draw, they wrote or drew. *Don't try to think or not to think,* I said. *Don't decide what to write or draw. Just let your hand do what it does and don't worry about it.*

Your nondominant hand responds to the hemisphere of your brain you use less often in daily communicative life. Using it without trying to edit or correct it allows that part of your mind to speak that usually can't get in a word edgewise. We don't write or draw very "well" with our nondominant hand, as you know if you've ever injured your dominant one and had to make do with the other. But truth isn't always about doing it well. Truth just has things it wants to say sometimes, and this little exercise gives it a chance.

One woman wrote the word "anger." *I didn't think I was angry,* she said. Many people drew circles. One drew an egg. A couple drew tears. A few wept. One man wrote "vengeance." Several people wrote "hope"; two women drew sunsets. Or maybe a sunrise, they couldn't say which. A couple of people wrote "fear," and one woman wrote "despair." Q drew the open doors of St. Clement's, our old parish.

Young people in the corner chopped up the papers with a paper cutter. We took them in a box out to the memorial garden, where we formed a circle, said a prayer for the dead, and sang the first verse of "America the Beautiful." Then we each buried a few skinny slips of the paper at the bases of the plants in the garden, where many peoples' ashes already have lain for a while, gradually becoming part of the soil and the plants and the trees. The ashes and the paper slips and the leaves from the trees become one thing. And that one thing is the stuff of life.

We stood in the garden as the sunshine dappled through the leaves of the trees, not quite wanting to leave. It was sunshine like the sunshine on that Tuesday the year before, that Tuesday that is becoming a part of us little by little, as we are able to receive it back into our spirits. It is making us what we are. We will never be the same. Nothing is ever the same. But we will be alive until we are dead, and even then we will continue to bring life to life.

This is how God renews the earth: through us. Through our ideas and actions, yes. But also through our bodies and the bodies of the beings who cannot be said to have ideas at all, all the atoms of all of us, after all thought has ceased. God uses all of it. Nothing can separate us. And nothing is lost.

The bulbs nestle down into the bottom of their new homes, pleasantly surprised to encounter the nutrients. Bulbs love bone meal, and everybody loves worm turds. The bulbs start to grow immediately. Within a few hours the roots have begun to move and change.

A season of hardship is essential for the bulbs. The worst thing that could happen to them would be to embark upon a warm, sweet season of high temperatures, abundant rain, and lovely warm sun. That's why you plant them now, in the fall. They need a season of cold, a time that looks like death. Gardeners who live in warm places have to put their bulbs in the icebox for a spell, to simulate the hardship the bulbs need. They need to be entombed for a while. Then they must feel the silent signal of a spring nobody else knows about yet, and the green hope in their hearts will prompt their first faint struggles up from the cold ground and into the light.

The bulbs look dead as I dig the holes and put them in. I think a sermon on them as I work: you would never know of your own strength were it not for your times that look like death. You would never hear the silent signal of your own hidden spring; you would never need to hear it. You would never know of your need for God. The worst thing that could happen to you would be to live permanently in the sunny meadows of good times. There is no strength to be won there.

Two hours of stretching and kneeling and digging, and I am one large ache. I look into the carton: there are still at least fifty bulbs left. I haven't even planted half of them.

If you could stand here where I'm standing and just hold the branch back out of the way, that would be good, Q says, pointing at an evergreen. His pointed shovel is already in the ground and has described a cautious circle around the rose bush we're going to move. It hasn't been thriving for the last couple of years, and I've talked him into relocating it to the sunny front garden. A certain breeziness in my approach to horticulture, though, makes him want to do the digging himself. I think he's afraid I might just pull the rose up out of the ground and walk away with it. I can understand that. *I want to get as many of the roots as I can,* he says. Oh.

I hold the prickly evergreen out of his way and watch him work. This is turning out to be a major job. There are really three canes, now, to the tree rose, as it has desperately tried to survive by sending up reinforcements to find the sun and secure nourishment from the competing evergreen roots all around it. The sun begins to sink in the west as Q continues to penetrate the soil with the shovel and pry the root ensemble up, up, a fraction of an inch at a time, freeing more and more of it from its grip on the earth.

At last it emerges: the three canes, each with its tap root and filament roots branching from it, and then the twisted old stump of the original rose, thick and gnarled and interesting. Maybe I'll wash the soil off it and display it on the mantel for a while. We trundle around front, shovels and trowels and clippers and roses and buckets of compost, and Q fights the ivy for space to accommodate the rose. This, too, is a significant effort. *We really should have cleaned it all out at once,* he says, in a mild rebuke of another example of my insouciance. He is right, of course. *I didn't want a bare space with nothing in it,* I counter, although the truth is that I am simply too lazy to do more than the minimum needed at the time. I'm a low-impact gardener.

Do we really need to add compost? I ask. *I think the soil looks great. The ivy kept it loose.* I am impatient to be finished. This is ungracious of me, as he is doing all the work and I am just standing there holding a rosebush.

It's all clay, he says. *It'll never do for roses.* Q withdraws the shovel and I see the wall of soil where it was. It is slick and smooth, like a pot. Clay.

Oh, I say, feeling like a ten-year-old. Q sifts compost carefully into the hole he has cleared of ivy roots, alternating it with small amounts of the soil. Then he settles the rose into it, filling in compost and soil in tiny handfuls all around the root. Finally he lets me water it and feeds it, and I water it again and we pack up and go in. I sneak out later and plant some beets, throwing the seeds messily into the soil and spreading a hasty layer on top of them. After the intricacies of the rose project, I should be ashamed, but somehow I am not. If they grow, they grow. If not, not.

Earlier in the day, he went to the store. *Get some balloons,* I said as he was leaving. *Red ones. For the hummingbirds.* What hummingbirds? We don't have any hummingbirds.

He came back with a shiny red balloon shaped like a star. He climbed out on the roof. Q has promised me that he won't go up on the roof any

more unless I'm home. I fear coming home late at
night and finding his corpse in the mint bed. He
affixed the balloon string to a hook he had screwed
into the wooden molding under the eaves. Then
he rigged a cord to be a pulley, so I can haul the
hummingbird feeder up and down to fill it. The
balloon bobs energetically in the breeze. My hope
is that a hummingbird will see it and think it's a
red flower. Then she'll fly down to our feeders.
Maybe she'll like it so much here she'll never
leave. We have a hummingbird paradise here, only
no hummers know about it yet.

We sit at dinner under the dogwood tree. I
have moved old hostas back here—the broad-
leaved shiny plants you see everywhere, mounding
from a central root, a hundred varieties with a
hundred different shades and patterns of foliage—
from their time-honored posts in front, where it
has just become too sunny and hot. Now they are
under the dogwood, where we also like to be in the
hot weather. A colony of shade-lovers has been
taking form gradually, refugees from hosta hell.
Certain folks here in town march the poor things
up and down along unshaded sidewalks. Why, I
couldn't tell you. They scorch and turn brown,
their flowers pathetic, short-lived spikes of valiant
pale lavender that turn the color of dust in one day
under that solar attack. But they are home under

the tree; down into the earth they stretch their toes, and I can tell by looking at them that it feels just wonderful.

We are thinking now about things to plant in their places out front. Drought-loving things. There are many such plants. But not hostas. And not astilbes, either, and not violas and not bleeding hearts. I have moved them all. Under the dogwood is going to be a very pretty place next summer.

The dryness has made the leaves begin to fall prematurely. They just gave up. *I say the hell with it,* one tree said to another one day last week, and they all began to let go.

We toast the rose bushes. Out of the corner of my eye, I can see the balloon, reflecting the light of our candles in the dark. I'm not used to seeing something moving around up by the roof. *It looks really silly,* I say, and he nods. The hummers may not come. The roses may not grow. Transplanting, even careful transplanting like Q does, is traumatic to a plant. We may not have roses out front. But we don't have roses out front right now, and are certain not to if we never put any in. So nothing is lost by trying. The balloon may not lure a hummingbird, but we don't have a hummingbird now, so we will have lost nothing by trying. If you never try, you're certain never to succeed. If you do try, you still may not. But then again, you may.

Let's go over there, I say to Q after dinner. We sit
in semidarkness under the dogwood tree, our plates
on the ground for the cats to lick. *Let's lie on the
ground over there. Nobody can see us.* And nobody
can. We lie down within a half-circle of evergreens
and gaze at the sky. It is stippled with the dark
shapes of leaves in the twilight, black against a silver sky. The sky viewed through the branches of
trees is a lovely, lacy thing to behold. We stay there
until the pattern of the leaves disappears into the
blackness of the night, and then we go inside.

And in the night, rain comes. Lovely, steady
rain, at last. I heard it on the roof, several times,
when I awoke to listen for a moment and then
drift off again. Lovely. And again today, rain. The
kind you want, the kind that falls for a long time in
a steady stream, not too hard and not too soft,
soaking into the earth and releasing the nutrients
in the soil to the tiny roots yearning to receive
them. We have longed for rain throughout this
hot, dry summer. Everyone in the garden is ready,
and all anyone wants is rain.

You can prepare. You can plant. You can prune
and fertilize and cultivate, but much of what happens in a garden is not up to you. This is why the
garden has been such a consistent literary and
devotional metaphor for life: it is what you make it,
but it is not just what *you* make it. Things happen

in it that you do not author. Gardening is learning to accept that and bend with it.

Like living. Today I will rake some of the leaves that have begun to fall and put them near, but not on, the compost pile. Q likes to arrange it himself. What the leaves will be like this year, I cannot say. The drought means all bets are off. But they will come again next year, after these have all decomposed and done their work. While the earth remains, the cycle will continue.

Fed Up

✿

"**M**anicurepedicure?" the young Korean woman asks, as if it were all one word. I nod, and Rosie goes off to get our boxes. We regulars all have personalized boxes at the nail place, each marked with our names and birth dates, so all I have to do is go to the shelf of March boxes to find mine. In each box are our own emery board, our own emery foot sponge, and our own orangewood stick.

Rosie and I meet back at the display of nail polishes, the little glass pots glowing like rows of jewels on the shelves. They are grouped by color, from the bright reds through the dark wines, the purply pinks all together, fading toward the pale

pinks and beiges. The odd golds, acid greens, and
cobalt blues stand out like . . . well, like sore
thumbs, a term not used lightly in this setting.
Rosie always matches her fingers to her toes. I
tend not to, preferring to show the world a modest
light shade and keep my wicked toes to myself.

Sometimes Rosie goes French, which costs a
little more. Art imitates nature in a French manicure: the tip of the nail is painted white, and the
bed is painted the color of an ordinary nail. Then
why bother, Q wants to know, if what you end up
with is a nail that looks like you didn't put anything on it? If you have to ask, I tell him, just never
mind.

*You should come with us sometime and have your
feet done,* I tell him. *You'd like it.* Lately, he's been
complaining that his toenails are changing shape.
Oh, yes, I say knowledgeably, and reel off a couple
of other things that happen to nails as people age,
like getting thicker or developing ridges or sometimes suddenly changing the direction of their
growth, so that they point straight up toward the
sky, instead of forward. Truth. It happened to my
mother.

But Q doesn't want to go to the nail place, not
even when I tell him he could have his feet in a
warm whirlpool and sit in a vibrating chair that
would massage his spine, not even when I mention

that a pretty Korean woman would give him a shoulder and neck massage. No. I didn't really think he would. I know he thinks the whole nail thing is an extravagance.

This morning I chose "Intimate" for my fingers and "Italian Love Affair"—because who's going to know?—for my toes. Rosie got "Mystic Pink" on both. *My nails are growing, Mamo,* she says, showing me one hand, and so they are. She bit them a lot a few weeks ago, but that seems to be over now.

"Did I ever tell you about the time I painted your toenails when you were a baby?' I ask her.

Rosie opens her eyes wide. "No-o," she says, on a rising *tell-me-more* note.

"Yup. You were about a month old. Maybe two months."

"Wasn't that a little dangerous?" she asks dubiously.

"Nah. Nails never hurt anybody." I was watching Rosie that afternoon, and decided to surprise her mother and paint the ten tiny nails bright pink. Mommy was surprised, all right.

Most of the colors have names like "Intimate" and "Mystic Pink." Names like "Chantilly" and "Pink Lemonade" and "Mad About Mauve" and "Ballet Slippers." Names like "Wine With Everything" and "Cabernet." There was one a few years back, so dark a purple that it was really black, called "Vamp." In general, the colors of nail polish are intended to suggest either girlish delicacy or dangerous sexiness, which is why I was pleasantly surprised to come across one last winter called "Fed Up." *Fed Up!* "I'll take that one," I said.

In my imagination, the names of nail colors are supplied by manicurists, the women who actually do the nails. New shades are constantly coming out, and each one needs a tempting name. So the girls come up with frill after frill. "Lace and Pearls." "Sold Out Show." "Sandy Beach Peach." On and on with the sweet stuff, except for the manicurist who will forever have my heart, the one who suggested "Fed Up."

"What should I call this one, Maxine?"

"I don't give a damn what you call it. My neck's killing me."

"No, come on, this is the last one. What shall I call it?"

"Then name it after me. Call it 'Fed Up.'"

"Fed Up" is an innocent-looking, almost-nude pink. It looks like it could have easily been given a sweetie-pie name like all the others, but I guess somebody had had one too many sugarplums that day. "Fed Up" it was. I wore it throughout the late fall my last year in my last parish, at a time when my physical health was failing and my mental health wasn't far behind. I would sit at my desk tasting my own despair, and then I would catch sight of my nails. Fed Up. And I would feel a little better. At least *someone* knew.

I preached my Christmas Eve sermon that year about "Fed Up." About the nail salon. About the weary manicurists. About the time I saw an angry customer make one of them cry. About the nail polish colors and their cutesy names, and about the feeling of kinship I had upon discovering "Fed Up." I preached about the reality of what the first Christmas must have been like, about weary, bloated Mary. Even the Bible says she was "great with child," and you just don't know "great" until you're a day or two past your due date. About there being no place to stay because Joseph didn't make a reservation. About the life into which Jesus was born, a life like ours, a life in which you're often fed up. Mary must have been fed up. Who knows, maybe she wasn't always as sweet as we remember her being, and Joseph was fed up with *her.* He'd been through a lot, too, remember. *Life is hard,* Jesus comes to say. *Life is hard, but God is good.*

The nail place is open seven days a week. It's a friendly place, pretty in its way, maybe a little heavy on the hot pink, but bright and cheerful. They play soft rock music on a radio all day. They offer greetings in a soft singsong to everyone who comes in, sounding happy to see each of us. The staff is all Korean. Some of them are educated women, but lack the requisite level of English proficiency to work in their professions here. English proficiency and, perhaps, INS working papers. I don't ask. I remember a Russian manicurist in another shop who had been a biochemist back home.

Let's see, what do the manicurists earn? A manicure costs nine dollars. The house must get at least half of that, so we're down to $4.50. The manicure takes about twenty minutes. So she could do three in an hour. But she rarely does three in an hour, except at very busy times. Maybe two. So she makes about ten dollars an hour, maybe. I always tip a lot, because I'm not sure other people do.

The lady who made the manicurist cry thought her nails had been cut too short. I don't know where she was while they were being done, because she didn't say anything until the manicure was finished, and then she lit into the young woman like Grant through Richmond. Everyone else in the shop sat very still, shocked, pretending not to hear the woman rant. *Don't let that girl touch your nails,* she snarled at me. (I was next in line for a manicure.) *Bitch,* I thought, although I didn't say anything. I could feel my own heart pounding in sympathetic anger. I sat down opposite the accused, who sat quietly looking down at her desk and blinking back tears. I took off my rings and gave her my trembling hands.

She was like Mary, I thought, with her downcast eyes filled with tears. People like Mary can't bite back when somebody who is more powerful than they are is cruel to them. When soldiers marched her bleeding, half-naked son off to his terrible death, Mary followed behind with her friends. Nobody who was in charge would do anything to help her. I doubt if she even asked. Of course not. She knew nobody anywhere around could or would do anything to make it stop. So she stood and took it, because there was nothing else to do and she wasn't about to leave him.

We go to the nail place, Rose and I, sometimes when we're feeling a little sad, something she and I have in common. I took her as soon after her back surgery as she could ride in the car, and we brought a pillow from home so she could sit in the vibrating chair and do something that would make her feel pretty again. We find our boxes and choose our colors from among the gemlike little pots. The manicurists are invariably cheerful, even at seven o'clock on a Thursday night, when they've been bent over peoples' hands and crouched over peoples' feet all day. Thursday's the last day you can get the weekday price for a manicure and pedicure, and so they're always very busy on Thursdays. They sing their hellos to us in soft voices that sound to me like the voices of little girls.

I am feeling much better these days, thank you, but sometimes I get "Fed Up" just for old times sake. I think of Maxine, the imaginary manicurist who named "Fed Up." *God bless you, Max, wherever you are.* And of the young woman who cried and the bitter woman who made her cry. *Bless you, honey, and stay in school, you hear? And bless you, ma'am, and maybe you should think about seeing somebody professionally, and I don't mean a manicurist.* Of the Russian woman following the American dream and winding up doing nails instead of working as a chemist. *Bless you, and welcome to our country. Welcome. It will not always be like this.*

The Collegiality Wars

❀

"Couldn't you be just a little more collegial?" my husband wants to know. He asks me this fairly often, every time I do something without consulting him. I am trying very hard to do this less and less. I am trying to include him in my lightning decision making. But it goes against my grain: if I include him, my decisions won't be lightning any more. They'll be something else—glacial, maybe. Eternal.

You overresearch things, I tell him silently. *You overprepare. You obsess about details. You are virtually motionless.*

This is childish of me. Childish and unworthy. So is the guerilla warfare I conduct around the issues upon which we disagree. I order a set of sheets on the Internet, buy somebody a gift. Lend somebody money. Commit to a project that will involve the car we share, without asking if it's available. In my imagination, my right to do each of these things inflates in size, becomes a referendum on my autonomy, my adulthood. They become human rights issues.

But they're not human rights issues. They're petty turf wars, the Kemoy and Matsu of our life together. Wars he doesn't even known he's fighting.

Besides, the truth is that I under prepare. I shoot from the hip. I count on my demonstrated ability to turn on a dime and pull a rabbit out of a hat. Sometimes it works. And sometimes it doesn't. When it doesn't, I grow defensive, casting about for someone to blame. I declaim about the vanity of focusing on trivial things, wonder snidely if some people might not have better things to do than worry about minutiae, imply that really productive people (me) don't bother themselves with details.

I vow to change. I will listen to him. I will talk things over with him in advance. I won't surprise him. I won't act unilaterally. I won't.

I will not overfill the tea kettle with water.

I will not leave a sponge in the kitchen sink.

I will not say we can do something without checking first.

I didn't say I wouldn't buy a horse.

The horse was not, shall we say, a budgeted expense. But my granddaughter loved horses—what little girl does not?—and wanted one. Of course. I had always wanted one when I was a girl, and rode friends' horses every chance I got.

Certainly.

But this is terrible. It is, I think the most terrible thing I've ever done, and I've done some terrible things. But sometimes I long for the chance to do things the way I want to do them just because I want to do them that way. Without having to say why. Without having to worry about whether someone else will be annoyed.

I should have asserted this autonomy around sponges or tea kettles, not horses. I could have avoided the situation in which I now find myself: owning a horse my husband doesn't know about. How did it happen, exactly? I have repressed the memory of my subterfuge. I know that Madeline did not ask me flat out to buy her a horse; she would never ask for such a thing. I think I saw her looking at pictures in her horse book, talking about which of the beauties she would choose if she could have one, and something within me said,

Well, why not? Why should she just have to daydream? Why shouldn't I make her daydream come true, if I can? And I could.

If Madeline and her mother would do the research and find a suitable horse at an affordable price, I would buy it and board it. The research took a long time. It was painstakingly conducted by Madeline, who haunted the Internet daily. The search narrowed. They visited horse farms. They found Leo.

Leo Lonesome Dundee was a cream-colored Quarter Horse. He was seven years old. He was slow and gentle. That was two years ago. Leo hasn't speeded up any.

At the time, I was drawing a meager but steady paycheck. I could afford to buy Leo, and I could afford to board him. I could afford his shoes and his worm medicine. I could afford his saddle and bridle and his new blanket. I could afford Madeline's riding boots.

I could buy these things invisibly. My husband and I have two joint checking accounts, but we manage them separately. Lady Bird Johnson once remarked that she wouldn't share a checking account with the Archangel Gabriel, and I concur. Lady Bird must have had her little projects, too. Q and I will be able to get at each other's money if one of us dies, but otherwise, we leave each other alone.

Thus, the fat checks to the horse farm and the tack store went out unnoticed.

Then I retired and began to write full time. Even more meager, but no longer steady, my income races Leo's horseshoes and boarding fees to the bank every month. I usually win, but only by a nose. In significant ways, it no longer makes sense to do this.

And I still haven't told Q.

He knows Leo exists. They've met. He knows that Madeline rides no one but Leo. I bring him garbage bags of manure from the horse farm to add to the compost. He knows Leo is the horse Madeline loves most.

The only thing he doesn't know is that Leo is our horse.

What if I die suddenly? What if I drop dead and, after three or four months, the horse farmer calls to say *hey-long-time-no-check* and gets Q on the phone, which he assuredly will, since I won't be taking calls? This monumental failure of collegiality will tarnish my memory forever. *What else didn't she tell me?* he will wonder, imagining bigamous marriages, apartments in undisclosed locations, illicit lovers waiting for word. Ranchettes in New Mexico.

We married too late. I was too set in my ways. Now, I don't know how to be a partner. I absorb the benefits of being married and won't pay the price. I buy a horse instead.

Madeline loves to groom Leo. She loves to groom him more than she loves to ride him, I think. At Halloween, she bought him a cap to wear, with ear covers—his costume. She shampoos his lovely tail and cuts his mane across his forehead. She rests her cheek against his flank and strokes his heavy winter coat. He comes across the field to greet her when she comes to see him.

I have begun to tell people. *You haven't told your husband?* a confidant asks in wonder. I shake my head and shrug. *I don't know what to do.*

I will leave this book out where he can find it. Maybe he doesn't read my stuff. If he gets to it, I'll confess. I was going to tell him, I'll say. I just never quite got around to it.

Just Now

The last day of another year. They grow shorter all the time: happy or painful, what they all have in common now is that they are fast.

I used to sit with my parents amid the ruins of a Christmas afternoon and lament the eons I would have to wait until the next Christmas. I would see them exchange an amused glance, amused, but in an odd way: full, also of pity, touched with sorrow. I did not understand that glance. It was one of those adult secrets.

But now I understand. From the front, life looks long, but only from the front. From the middle, it's a very short train.

Q and I attend the parish I first served twenty-two years ago as a young curate. Babies I baptized are in college now. Teenagers in my youth group are middle-aged. There are many people in the church I do not know; they came after my time. But many are still here, older, but the same. The Hallbauers bring some relatives to church: "I remember you," one says at the door as we shake hands, "I remember hearing you preach when you were young!"

I remember, too. I remember lots of things. Over the past year I have made a tremendous change in my ministry, leaving a beloved parish to make writing, spiritual direction, and retreat leading the center of my work. It was hard to make the change—I mourned St. Clement's for at least six months—but it has been made. Ministry goes on, but it changes over the years. Every change hurts a bit, but it happens nonetheless.

At the year's beginning, and most of the way through the year, I was still in shock from the bombing of the World Trade Center and absorbed in the recovery work that followed it. I was not alone in that. For most of the year, it was as if it were still happening, every day.

But, the other night, I sat at the dinner table and looked out onto the street, thinking about it, and I realized that something in me had shifted, that the bombing was now in the past for me, that it had taken its place there without my knowing. I still feel my stomach lurch when I see twisted metal of any kind, or when I hear a siren, or an explosion of any kind. Perhaps I always will. But the bombing itself has happened. Not that I have let it go: it's not going anywhere. Maybe what I have done, rather, is let it come. Come into my history, and stay there as part of me.

And now we are at war. Someday we will not be. Make it soon.

Things become past. History only moves forward. Yet we proclaim God as the Lord of history, containing it, yet not contained by it. We need our pasts and presents and our futures here, but God contains all of those and needs none of them. In the realm of God, there is no time. The things we struggle to bring into order within us are all present within God.

The World Trade Center stands straight and tall, its thousands of people busily at work in their offices. Mount Vesuvius stands, beautiful in the distance, a majestic, benign presence to the people of Pompeii on a bright, sunny day. Thomas Becket prepares to celebrate the Mass. The Jews of Warsaw awaken and begin another day, secure in their homes, their breakfasts cooking on the stoves. An African man looks up and sees a great ship with white sails, one like he's never seen before making for the land, and wonders what manner of people are coming. He goes to investigate. Later his friends find his spear.

He and his friends, the Jews, the people of Pompeii, the people in the offices that day in a New York September, all live in God. What happened to them lives there, and what happened after. And what happened before. And even, perhaps, what might have happened. There is no time with God. That probably makes heaven a pretty strange place.

Strange, but only to us. When we are there, it will be as if we had always been there. There will be no next, or tomorrow, or yesterday. Just now.

The sun begins to rise: another day. Here we have days; there they do not need them. Another year of days has ended, and a new one begins. Love the days that unfold, for you will never have them, again, not here. But God has them all.